Historic
SOUTH END
HALIFAX

D1239741

IMAGES *of our Past*

HISTORIC
SOUTH END HALIFAX

PETER McGUIGAN

NIMBUS
PUBLISHING

Dedication

In memory of Dr. Cyril Byrne (1940–2006), professor of English and founder of the Irish Studies Department at Saint Mary's University.

Nimbus Publishing Limited
PO Box 9166
Halifax, NS B3K 5M8
(902) 455-4286

Printed and bound in Canada

Design production: Margaret Issenman
Cover: Heather Bryan
Title Page: Golden Gates at Young Avenue

Library of Canada Cataloguing in Publication Data

McGuigan, Peter T.
Historic South End Halifax / Peter McGuigan.
ISBN 13: 978-1-55109-602-5
ISBN 10: 1-55109-602-1

1. Halifax (N.S.)—History. I. Title.
FC2346.52.M34 2007   971.6'225   C2007-902903-5

We acknowledge the financial support of the Government of Canada through the Book Publishing Industry Development Program (BPIDP) and the Canada Council, and of the Province of Nova Scotia through the Department of Tourism, Culture and Heritage for our publishing activities.

Contents

Acknowledgements

The Dalhousie University Archives had a considerable number of photos from Halifax in general, including some aerial shots from the early 1930s showing much of the South End. I would like to thank Karen Smith. Dalhousie's Special Collections also had many useful dissertations.

Saint Mary's University had few old photos, as they only started their archives in the 1990s. Still, I found several aerial shots showing the Gorsebrook Golf Course and the South End.

Hansel Cook is the archivist. At Saint Mary's, Mrs. Hanka Hudka produced a list of their dissertations.

Thanks to the Spring Garden Road Public Library staff and Joanne McCarthy, the research librarian.

The Army Museum in the Citadel had dozens of photographic binders. They hold a number of Victorian-era photographs from Point Pleasant Park and several military photos from World War II. Miriam Walls was very helpful.

The Nova Scotia Sports Hall of Fame had photos and short biographical outlines of the athletes mentioned in the text and the Maritime Command Museum supplied a photo of Rear Admiral Murray. Thanks to Marilyn Gurney for her assistance.

Finally, at Nova Scotia Archives and Records Management, Philip Hartling showed me the ropes for the photograph collection. Then there was Gary Shutlack, the senior duty archivist. Even when not on the desk, he often took a few minutes to look for something that twigged his interest. He also read the text and made several suggestions. Thanks to both people and to the rest of the NSARM staff.

Several people not yet mentioned must also be thanked. Dr. Allan Marble of the Dalhousie Medical Department read the hospital material, making a number of useful suggestions. I must also thank my late cousin, Dr. Cyril Byrne, recently retired from the Saint Mary's English Department, for offering to check the text for style. He had just received the first chapter when he was diagnosed with brain cancer. Cyril died August 17, 2006.

Finally, I must thank my mother, Stella Healey, and my former neighbours, the late Margaret Martin and Elizabeth Hartling, for their memories, especially of World War II. Then there are three others who also contributed. Dr. Fred Matthews made observations on society in general, and David Freeman, another old neighbour, and Don Wright, a current neighbour, contributed their South End remembrances.

Any remaining errors are mine.

Introduction

The Mi'kmaq called Halifax "Chebucto," meaning "biggest harbour." Although little is known of early Mi'kmaq settlements in the South End, it is believed Mi'kmaq wintered inland and moved to the shores of the harbour, particularly to the area now comprising Point Pleasant Park, in the summer. Europeans did not permanently settle Halifax until its founding in 1749. The military town, and in particular the Citadel, was to be the English counter-balance to the French fortress of Louisbourg in Cape Breton. Throughout the eighteenth century the town's population rose and fell in accordance with English military campaigns. While the fortress at the Citadel soon became the centre of the town, the far south end of the peninsula was of strategic importance for its views to the mouth of the harbour, and military installations soon appeared in what is now Point Pleasant Park.

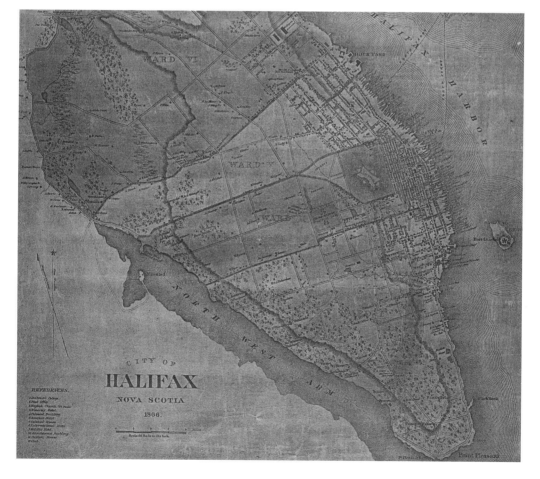

The centre of the small town was at first surrounded by a palisade. Outside the wall, surveyor Charles Morris planned two suburbs with more spacious lots for farms. Immediately north of the palisade was the North Suburb, reaching for the modern North Street. Immediately south of the palisade, the South Suburb spread toward the modern South Street. The South Suburb was marine oriented from the start, and its citizens included the economic elite, who traded with the West Indies and New England, allowing them to build stone homes on Hollis Street, not far from the harbour. Along Water Street were the houses of the fishers and stevedores, who also worked in the South Suburb, but at a marginal income.

Only about 2,500 British originally came with Cornwallis to Halifax. New England Planters soon followed, largely settling in the Annapolis Valley and defining Nova Scotia as the fourteenth colony. Following Britain's shattering 1783 defeat in America, thousands of Loyalists also settled in Nova Scotia, with many remaining in Halifax. Irish Catholics from Britain's western isle and Newfoundland also arrived in the city, settling in the South Suburb on Water Street, their distinct "wild Irish" speech soon marking the South Suburb as "Irishtown." As the two suburbs, south and north, continued to expand, they became increasingly distinct, a distinction that became more pronounced with the founding of several universities and hospitals in the South End.

Although the boundaries are arbitrary, peninsular Halifax's South End is generally considered to be the area south of Quinpool Road, Bell Road, and Sackville Street. The South End is said to be wealthy, just as the West End is said to be middle class and the North End is imagined as working class. Like many generalizations, this is honoured more in the breach than in the observance. Yes, the South End has million-dollar homes, a semi-exclusive boat club, at least one private residential road, and a nearly gated community. But it is also slashed by the railway cut, has lost the fashionable end of Pleasant Street (now Barrington), and contains several less affluent neighbourhoods. The South End may be wealthier on average than other sections of the peninsula, but its people and its history are far more complicated and diverse than the stereotype of the "wealthy South End" might suggest.

This diversity helps explain, in part, why Halifax's South End is often conceptualized as a series of neighbourhoods. These neighbourhoods became further defined when the railway cut, completed in 1918, geographically isolated parts of the southern end of the peninsula. These neighbourhoods include the original portion of the South Suburb (originally marked by South Street); the downtown and commercial core, represented most prominently by Spring Garden Road and the southern portions of Barrington Street; the two small neighbourhoods originally founded along ethnic lines, Irishtown and Schmidtville; the "new" South End near the Northwest Arm, at one time the town's premier vacation area featuring several grand estates; and the "old" West End, the area defined by Quinpool Road, Robie Street, South Street, and the Arm.

With the largest Canadian commercial district on the east coast, Spring Garden Road, a fine Public Gardens, a massive container pier and ocean terminals, several of Nova Scotia's finest hospitals and universities, and a once-strategic military installation (now a grand public park) at Point Pleasant, the history of Halifax's South End is as fascinating and distinguished as the people who live there.

Chapter 1

The South Suburb, Irishtown

IRISHTOWN, 1887, LOOKING SOUTHEAST FROM THE SAINT MARY'S CATHEDRAL STEEPLE.

The 1752 census shows 765 inhabitants in the North Suburb and 818 individuals in the South Suburb. There were 2,032 other individuals within the pickets, most of whom were English. Adding 195 people in Dartmouth, 216 on the rest of the largely wooded peninsula, and 202 fishers on islands and harbour islands, Halifax totalled about 4,248 citizens. This figure would vary wildly with the fortunes of war, at least for its first half-century.

In the South Suburb, the small number of Irish-born grew slowly until 1815, but they left their mark. Speaking their distinctive "Wild Irish," they

His Excellency
Captain General & Governour in Chief
Massachuset's Bay & New Hampshire
&c. Admiral

JONATHAN BELCHER Esq
of His Majesty's Provinces of
the New England
&c. the same

**CHIEF JUSTICE
JONATHAN
BELCHER**

gave streets like Tobin and Fawson their own family names. Also, starting in 1785, the Catholic clergy and later bishops associated with Halifax were typically Irish, creating a long line of Irish religious figures. Finally, when the first Saint Mary's Cathedral was finished in 1829, it was built in the Irish Georgian Gothic style, yet another example of the Irish influence in the city.

In the photo of Irishtown, 1887, the better residences, including the Lieutenant Governor's in the lower right, are on Pleasant Street (Barrington) and on south Hollis, while the slums are on the waterfront facing the wharves. Immediately west of south Hollis Street, the Irish influence was also felt, particularly at John Murphy's large rocky farm on Fort Massey Hill. Murphy was one of the earliest Irish Catholics to arrive in the city, in 1749, and became one of the founders of Saint Peter's, the town's first Catholic church. His farm was bounded on the north by modern Harvey Street, on the south by Smith Street, and west and east by Queen and Pleasant Streets.

As the number of Irish increased, a tragedy unfolded that would have an important effect on the religious climate of the province. In 1755 Governor Charles Lawrence suddenly expelled the Acadians, who had refused to sign an unconditional treaty of loyalty. Lawrence then brought "Planters" (pre-loyalists) from New England to occupy the vacated land. However, the Planters, who were used to the tradition of American democracy with its local autonomy, forced Lawrence to call an assembly. It met for the first time on June 3, 1757. This legislature, now celebrated by the Memorial Tower on the Northwest Arm, also reflected another eighteenth-century American tradition: anti-Catholicism. The legislature quickly imposed disabilities on the small Catholic minority. Papists were forbidden to own property, vote, sit in the legislature, or have priests. Nine years later, the legislature also forbade Catholic schools and teachers. Catholics were to be kept ignorant, without property, and impoverished. Fortunately, the political reality was stronger than the prejudices in what was, for a time, the fourteenth colony.

The precipitating event to the end of anti-Catholicism was the collapse of French influence in North America and the resulting willingness of the Mi'kmaq to come to terms with the English. Led by their Catholic priest and translator, Father Pierre Maillard, "apostle to the Micmac," and their chief, Argimault, the Mi'kmaq met Chief Justice Jonathon Belcher in the Governor's Garden, immediately above the town cemetery, in July 1761. Argimault literally "buried the hatchet" before the assembled dignitaries.

OLD SAINT MARY'S CATHEDRAL AND GLEBE, C.1868

Maillard's acceptance as a translator was the beginning of the end of legal anti-Catholicism in Nova Scotia. Governor Lawrence, despite the assembly, had brought Maillard to Halifax in 1760 to minister to the Acadians held on George's Island and the Mi'kmaq lurking in the nearby forests. This priest became so vital that Lawrence took him into his confidence, even giving him a pension. Maillard was allowed to say mass, apparently in John Murphy's barn on Fort Massey Hill. Unfortunately, Maillard died on August 12, 1762, not long after arriving in the province. As there was no Catholic cemetery, Maillard was buried by his Anglican friend, Rev. Thomas Wood, in the town graveyard, now St. Paul's, at Barrington and Spring Garden. Assembled were government dignitaries, members of his oratory at Murphy's, and sorrowful Mi'kmaq. By the 1780s, the rise of a small Irish-Catholic middle class meant anti-Catholicism was failing.

The adjacent building in the photo is the girls' school, established in 1820 and later called Saint Mary's.

SAINT MARY'S GOTHIC BASILICA UNDER RECONSTRUCTION, C.1875

Having ingratiated themselves by reserving seats at Saint Paul's Anglican Church and by their willingness to marry Anglicans, the Halifax Catholic elite requested permission for a new priest and for permission to erect a church. In 1784 this was granted, and they purchased the property where Saint Mary's Cathedral is today. There, they established the first church in the South End, St. Peter's Chapel. This small, red wooden chapel faced Grafton Street, with its graveyard in the present parking lot of the basilica. The first Saint Mary's Cathedral was started by the city's first Roman Catholic bishop, Edmund Burke, on May 24, 1820. It was completed nine years later after his death in November 1829. The cathedral was replaced in the mid-1870s by a gothic basilica, pictured under construction.

GOVERNMENT HOUSE, C.1860

Diagonally across Pleasant from the St. Mary's glebe was Government House, a very large Neo-Classical or Georgian home. The occupants, Governor Wentworth and Lady Frances, did not pay poll tax, but had severely taxed the protesting assembly. Caught between demands for roads and the endless appeals for a grand governor's house, the assembly capitulated to Wentworth. After all, it was argued, most of the material to build the house would come from within the colony. In 1799 the assembly approved over ten thousand pounds towards construction, believing this would be enough to finish the building. It wasn't. Wentworth refused to surrender economic control to the assembly. The members then faced the terrible choice of either surrendering or getting a half-finished building of no use to anyone. Ultimately, the assembly kept doling out funds, the stone construction being the chief reason for overruns. Government House's final cost was about thirty thousand pounds, an enormous sum that indicates the Wentworths' desire for a late eighteenth-century English country estate.

Even before the South Suburb was becoming fashionable, "the Mall" was created in 1766 by planking a sidewalk from Saint Paul's Church to the Freshwater Bridge (the corner of Inglis and Pleasant). The bridge was known as the "Kissing Bridge," and beloved by the young, who carved their names on the rails. Soon the trail, though not the boardwalk, was extended along Inglis Street, Tower Road, and Spring Garden Road, before circling back to Pleasant. Those in their finery, with a carriage or a sulky, enjoyed being seen, and in the early 1800s the citizens would even see the Duke of Kent and his entourage. Meanwhile, the development of Pleasant Street continued. As early as 1775 there were market gardens at the southeast corner of Pleasant and Morris that lasted almost a century. Housing in the early 1800s was scattered along Pleasant and Hollis Streets. Travelling south along Pleasant from Salter, the first home was the very grand Government House.

GOVERNOR JOHN
WENTWORTH, N.D.

Wentworth was replaced as governor in 1808 and reluctantly given a pension by the legislature. Eventually, the Wentworths moved back to England, settling near the royal palace. When Frances died, Wentworth, now old, returned to a Halifax he hardly knew. The former governor of New Hampshire died at age 83 on April 8, 1820.

BISHOP CHARLES INGLIS, C.1787

Near Morris Street on the west side of Pleasant Street was the large Inglis family cottage. Here lived two Anglican bishops, Charles "Paddy" Inglis and John Inglis, and John's son, Sir John Inglis, the hero of Lucknow who later had Inglis and Lucknow Streets named for him. Born in Ireland, Paddy became the first Anglican bishop of Nova Scotia and founded King's College.

Below South Street was Jimmy Fitzgerald's farm that covered most of the late John Murphy's property on Fort Massey Hill. The place was so well known that it was simply called the "Fitzgerald Farm." There were twenty acres "in the highest state of cultivation," and several improvements, including a house and barns. To the immediate south, Fitzgerald also had thirty acres of pasture that almost reached the Freshwater Bridge. (Little did Fitzgerald dream that nine speculators would later sell his property for twenty thousand pounds and that today it would be worth millions.)

CHARLES MORRIS HOUSE, C.1840

Charles Morris, chief surveyor of the province who also planned the layout of Charlottetown, built the two wooden houses below Hollis. Further south, Hollis had some other fine homes. The Honourable John Black's big Georgian stone house was built about 1819. At least part of the material probably came from Scotland on his ships. Black's house is now crowded by other buildings, but once stood in splendid isolation. A large garden was later sold to Saint Matthew's for their fine church. The large lot in front would eventually be taken over by Alexander Keith's brewery. Black was a senior member of Black, Forsythe, and Company, a West Indian Trading Company.

Those who lived on Water Street did so to be close to the harbour. With their homes mostly on the west side, and the wharves and West Indian and New England trading companies on the east, the workers were conveniently located. Many residents were mariners, so were often away on long voyages. Others were stevedores and worked the docks. Women and children worked cutting and cleaning fish, or as servants in the wealthier homes.

**HALIFAX LADIES'
COLLEGE,
PLEASANT STREET,
1896**

The Ladies' College was the Protestant analogue of the Catholic Convent of the Sacred Heart, an elite school designed to produce cultured young women who would make suitable wives for the well-to-do. The College was established by Saint Matthew's Church in the Uniacke/Duffus home at Harvey Street and Pleasant in 1887, almost two generations after the convent opened. The Uniacke/Duffus property was beautifully treed, with a large set-back building. The college eventually moved to Oxford Street, taking over John T. Wylde's big home "Armbrae" in 1940.

THE WILLIAM A. HENRY HOUSE, N.D.

On the next block from the original Ladies' College was William Alexander Henry's stone house, number 158, dating from 1829. Henry, born in northern Ireland, was a "Father of Confederation" and Supreme Court judge, whose formal education was limited to high school. He switched his political allegiance from Liberal to Tory in 1857 when Joseph Howe drove the Catholics from the Liberals. Henry died in 1888.

Saint Matthew's Presbyterian Church, c.1900

The most prominent building on the east side of Pleasant Street was Saint Matthew's Church, next to the Lieutenant Governor's grand home. Saint Matthew's was a Gothic masterpiece with its centred, sharply pointed steeple, strongly pitched roof, and pointed windows, reminiscent of praying hands. It was built uptown after the burning of Mather's Meeting House on January 1, 1857. Legislation following the fire had forbidden large wooden buildings in downtown Halifax, so Saint Matthew's was rebuilt in stucco-covered brick. The result was a beautiful Victorian building and the second church in Irishtown. Opened October 20, 1859, it also featured a thirty-metre spire.

ERNEST LAWSON,
1930

Living in Saint Matthew's old manse was Dr. Archibald Lawson. He was one of the best-known physicians in Halifax before he performed an illegal abortion. After his conviction in 1883, he fled to Mexico. His son, Ernest, born ten years earlier on Hollis, became a famous American Impressionist. Ernest Lawson drowned in 1939 off Coral Gables, Florida. His impression of Harlem River was such a favourite of the White House that Nancy Regan later borrowed it from the Metropolitan Museum of Modern Art.

SIR EDWARD KENNY HOUSE, 1931

Born poor in County Cork, Ireland, Edward Kenny and his brother Thomas were apprenticed as clerks to James Lyons. After Lyons came to Halifax in the 1820s, the Kennys followed, with Edward working for Lyons and Thomas establishing T. Kenny Company. In 1827 Edward joined his brother's company. Edward, a Liberal, later supported Confederation and served in Ottawa as a member of the Privy Council. He and his wife, the beautiful Ann Forrestal, had a large number of children, including two well-known religious figures. Father George Kenny, a Jesuit, became president of Fordham University. Unhappy for much of his life, he felt it was impossible to live a holy life while among humanity. His sister, Mother Ellen Kenny, became the superior of the Convent of the Sacred Heart.

Benjamin Weir was the chief agent of the southern American Confederacy in Halifax. His opponent was the local United States Council member, Mortimer M. Jackson. The American government easily broke the Confederate cipher and intercepted Weir's mail. Weir, however, got his revenge. In December 1863 Confederate agents seized the American steamer *Chesapeake* and brought it into Halifax Harbour, killing an officer in the process. Trailing American cruisers had forced the ship into Halifax harbour and then entered the harbour themselves without much resistance, since the British fleet normally stationed there was wintering in Bermuda. The British army commander in Halifax, Sir Charles Hastings Doyle, kept things calm, at least until the chief suspect, George Wade, was brought ashore. As Wade stood on the wharf, a boat approached the pier. The boatmen suddenly hustled Wade aboard and pulled away quickly. A plainclothes police officer, Lewis Hutt, drew his gun and ordered the vessel to stop. He was disarmed by three of Halifax's other pro-Confederates: Dr. William Johnston Almon, Alexander Keith, and Dr. P. W. Smith. The trial of the three failed to produce convictions—they were simply too high-ranking to pay for their crimes in a city so riven by political differences. Bejamin Weir's home was on Hollis Street.

KEITH'S BREWERY, 1892

The cornerstone for the Keith's brewery on Lower Water Street was laid June 17, 1837. Alexander Keith prospered after slave labour was eliminated by Britain in 1833 and the price of rum soared. Born into a well-to-do family, he learned the brewing trade in England before coming to Halifax in the early 1820s. He twice served as the city's mayor, and was a well-known Confederate supporter during the American Civil War.

STEPHEN TOBIN AND WIFE, C.1875

At the corner of South and Pleasant was the big estate of former mayor Stephen Tobin, built in 1830. His grandparents had emigrated from Ireland about 1820 and had accumulated a large property on Fort Massey Hill. Tobin Street commemorates them. Stephen, son of Maggie Synnott and Thomas Tobin, was first elected as mayor in 1867. His 1868 marriage to Catherine Lyons Grey was a civic event. The ceremony at Saint Mary's Cathedral was followed by the ringing of both church and fire station bells. City council offered congratulations at City Hall, and Halifax was gay with bunting. In the evening, the law courts on Spring Garden were illuminated. This celebration was an incredible turn-around from the previous year's election when, as a pro-Confederation candidate, he was defeated. Tobin was mayor from 1867–69 and 1878–80.

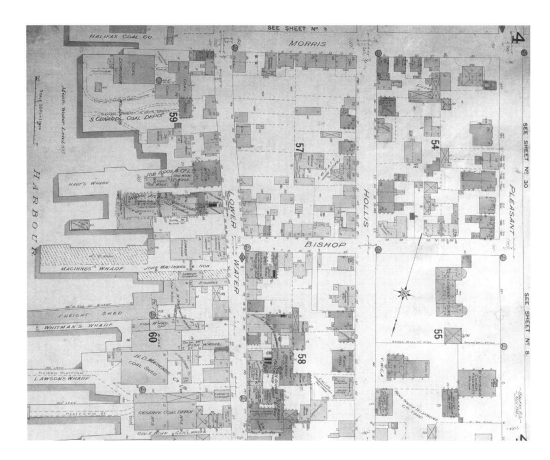

IRISHTOWN AFTER 1890, 1914 FIRE INSURANCE MAP

A report on city tenements that appeared in the January 7, 1890 *Herald* described several decrepit buildings in Irishtown. The buildings suffered from rotten foundations and floors, defective sanitation systems, and were generally out of repair.

By 1914, the Ocean Terminals and the Canadian National Railways had taken over the area southeast of South and Hollis, the old Royal Engineers Yard. Lower South Street, including the run-down Tobin estate, would later be demolished for Cornwallis Park. With the construction of the Ocean Terminals, there was money to be made providing temporary rooms with meals included. As a result, boarding houses were taking over from grand old homes. Esson's home at South and Pleasant was the Elmwood Boarding Home, and Weir's home at Hollis and Fawson had become the Grosvenor's Boarding Home. The city's first hotels also appeared with the railroad. The Lord Nelson was the city's first hotel and was associated with CP. The CN hotel, the Nova Scotian, was Halifax's second modern hotel. Both hotels, however, struggled during the Depression.

THE NOVA SCOTIAN HOTEL, 1931

The 1951 Fire Insurance Map shows the Capitol Theatre at the site of the 1877 Academy of Music. The Nova Scotia Telephone Company, now calling itself the Maritime Telephone and Telegraph Company, was pushing toward Barrington. Black's Hollis Street home had apartments. The new Navy League Building, on the east side of Hollis between Morris and South, had replaced its lost building at Pleasant and South. Hollis developed a number of flea-bag hotels, including the Acadian and the Cornwallis. Water Street had lost more houses. The southwest corner of Morris and Hollis had two big tanks belonging to Nova Scotia Light and Power. But Fawson's north side gained a number of government buildings, including the unemployment insurance office. On South and Barrington was the office of the Royal Canadian Air Force Eastern Command, the former Naval League Building. Further down Barrington, the Sisters of Service Home was at Tobin, once occupied by Sheriff Sawyer. Diagonally across the street was Cornwallis Park, formerly the Tobin Estate.

Irishtown, once a distinct area like Schmidtville and Dutch Town, has disappeared. The last media mention seems to have been in the *Commercial News* in 1958. More recently Irishtown has been repopulated by the young and well-to-do. Bishop's Gate on the boardwalk has helped bring the area back to prominence. Still, Local 269 of the International Longshoremen's Office is on Hollis, and Nova Scotia Power still uses part of its plant at the south end of Water Street. Unfortunately, there is little trace of the Irish. The Celtic Cross that memorializes the 1749 pioneers and their descendants' accomplishments is not even in Irishtown, but on George Street near the modern ferry terminal.

Irishtown featured some positive aspects. For example, the area long featured swimming, an indication of how clean the harbour was. An 1843 advertisement for sea bathing welcomed ladies and gentlemen, as well as families, and a female attendant was present during the ladies' hours. Swimmers only had to supply their own "bathing gown" and towel. The rates were 6s, 4d for adults, 5s for children, and 12s, 6d for families. Most times, however, the news from Irishtown was not good. For example, the south end of Hollis Street in the 1820s was not the best place to respect the Holy Day. There were several stone houses there, one occupied by a Colonel Creigh, and across the street, a house used by another military man, Cochrane. On Sunday evenings they would have one of the regiments play dance music from dusk until ten o'clock, drawing some respectables, but mostly the "great unwashed, who…made [it] hideous with their coarse jests and notorious conduct." This practice ended in 1828 when Governor Sir Peregrine Maitland arrived and Victorianized society.

There were also frequent reports of excessive drinking in Irishtown. The *Acadian Recorder* of September 10, 1872, reports the "Irish Town Riot." Stephen Rice, nineteen and drunk, interfered with stevedores at Phalen's Wharf on Salter Street. The foreman got the police. Seeing Rice in trouble, James Kennedy, twenty-six, came galloping to his rescue. Soon, however, he was in trouble with the police too, so gave what the paper called the "Kennedy battle cry." The only one who responded was James's foolish old man, Michael, fifty-five, whom the police also arrested. The court gave the three clowns the option of a fine or jail time. They all probably served time, as they were not likely able to afford the fines.

Chapter 2

Schmidtville, A German Area

AERIAL VIEW OF SCHMIDTVILLE FROM SAINT MARY'S STEEPLE, 1888.

S chmidtville, delimited by Spring Garden Road, Morris Street, Queen Street and Dresden Row, was the third part of the South End to be developed following the South Suburb and Spring Garden Road. Brenton Street, with its related houses and trades, can be seen as a Schmidtville extension. Schmidtville was one of three areas on the Halifax peninsula bearing German names. The other, better-known areas are Dutch Town in the North End and Dutch Village on the broad neck that makes the city a peninsula. The earliest German settlers to Schmidtville arrived in the 1790s, thirty years after settling Dutch Town and Dutch Village. While the Germans of Dutch Town and Dutch Village came from areas near the junction of Germany, Switzerland, and France, the founders of Schmidtville came from Saxony, near the Czech border, and Hesse, bordering on Holland.

Schmidtville probably received its name from a Loyalist, Captain Christian Wilhelm Schmidt of the Royal Foreign Artillery, who fought for King George III during the American Revolution. Born in Hesse–Rottenburg, Schmidt died in Halifax at seventy-four in 1828. The area was likely called Schmidtville after Schmidt's wife, Elizabeth Pedley, divided her late father's twelve acres into lots. Pedley's Fields, as the area had been known, started to be called Schmidtville. Not unexpectedly, both German and English street names appeared. The former Rottenburg Street, now Clyde, was named after Schmidt's home area. Dresden Row is supposed to have come from the city where James's wife originated.

JOE HOWE, C.1860

As a young boy, Joe Howe knew the Schmidtville area well. Although living on the Arm near Point Pleasant, he walked across the largely uninhabited peninsula to Rev. George Wright's school downtown. In 1837, Howe wrote in his "Western Rambles": "A few years ago there was not a single house in Schmidtville—it was then a decent sort of pasture. We used to meet an old man every morning…driving a solitary cow to the clover and buttercups. Had he told us in 1837…that it would contain nearly as many houses as Irish-town, a suspicion of insanity would have been induced." Yet, by the 1830s, houses were sprouting like the buttercups and clover.

In 1831 the area had only thirty-eight settlers, and not many were German. There were still many empty lots toward Morris Street. The assessment of 1834 shows the number of occupants had fallen to only fourteen, many of whom were new property owners. Among them was Captain Broke, whose property was worth 1,200 pounds, and Captain Rivers, whose property was valued at 450 pounds. They were probably stationed at nearby Bellevue House. All the other properties were of less value, including an apparently undeveloped property valued at only seventy-five pounds. Whatever happened, Mrs. Schmidt's investment seems to have gotten off to a slow start.

On May, 15, 1841, *The Acadian Recorder* reported a serious fire in Schmidtville. The fire started at painter Joey Metzler's house near Spring Garden Road at about 11:00 p.m. Several houses were connected to Metzler's. Mrs. Athol's on the north was burned to the ground, but on the other side, the fire at Bartholomew's was stopped on the roof. A severe shortage of water meant that several engine companies had to combine their hoses and run a line all the way from the Freshwater Stream. The settlement was saved, although three "handsome" houses were lost.

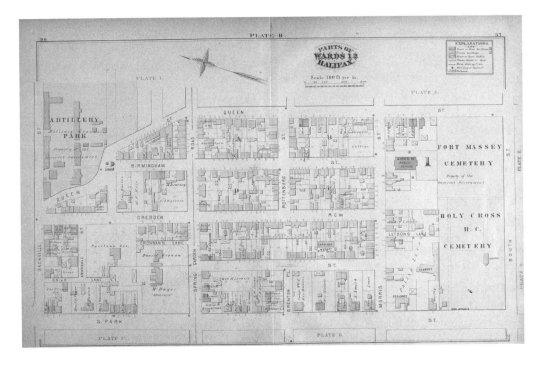

**HOPKINS ATLAS,
PLATE "H," 1914**

Hopkin's Atlas of 1878 showed the area having little commercial development, even on Spring Garden. There was only one brick house in Schmidtville, on Queen, near Rottenburg, that belonged to Edward Morrison of E. Morrison and Company, a flour, food, and corn company on the Market Wharf at George Street. The most prominent property owner in Schmidtville was Premier P. C. Hill, a distinguished graduate of King's College, who had a property at Morris and Queen. Almost as prominent was Rev. Dr. C. G. Gilpin who lived at 26 Spring Garden, near Birmingham. Gilpin was principal of the Halifax Grammar School on Birmingham. Despite little commercialization, there was a bakery near the southern end of Dresden Row, and M. J. O'Brien's Carriage Works on the east side of Brenton.

Schmidtville gradually grew, attracting semi-skilled and skilled workers. In the late 1870s they held positions such as gardeners, assistant
appraisers, undertakers, plasterers, blacksmiths, coachmen, shoemakers,
masons, bakers, milkmen, block makers, labourers, grocers, and bell
hangers. A number of Royal Army officers and other men from nearby
Bellevue still had houses in the area, as did several police officers who
lived on Birmingham.

The best known of the police officers was Nicholas Power, the chief
of police. An ex-Royal Navy man, he saved the life of King George V
when a terrorist tried to blow up the battleship HMS *Canada*. Power
received the George Medal in 1915. He lived on Dresden Row with
his wife, Alice Callaghan, and was still puttering around his garden at
ninety. Power finally died in 1938 at the age of 96.

**EDWARD GILPIN,
N.D.**

Paradoxically, the most important institution in Schmidtville was the elite Halifax Grammar School at number 59 Birmingham, just down from Spring Garden Road. Founded in 1789 at Barrington and Sackville Streets to teach traditional English high culture, including Latin and Greek, the "seminary" moved to Birmingham Street in 1865. Rev. Edward Gilpin was the fourth and longest-lasting principal. Born in Annapolis Royal in 1821, the son of Elizabeth and Dr. Edwin Gilpin, he was educated at King's College in Windsor, and received his BA in 1847. A year later he joined the Grammar School. By 1863 he had a Doctorate in Divinity and had become principal. Gilpin married Amelia Haliburton, daughter of "Sam Slick" creator, Judge Thomas Haliburton. They lived on Spring Garden Road just down a path which led to the school on Birmingham. Gilpin was also Dean of the Anglican cathedral, Saint Luke's, on Morris Street.

In 1877, a high school was authorized for each county. Halifax's was established at Sackville and Brunswick, and Gilpin was its first principal. In 1885 it became the Halifax County Academy, with girls admitted on the same conditions as boys. Four years later, Gilpin resigned, finally feeling his age. Students gave him a great send-off, and he was lauded for teaching generations culture, superior morals, and better qualities of intellectual and physical vigour. Over the next few years, Gilpin was often seen walking along Spring Garden in his cassock and low-crowned hat. He died in 1906.

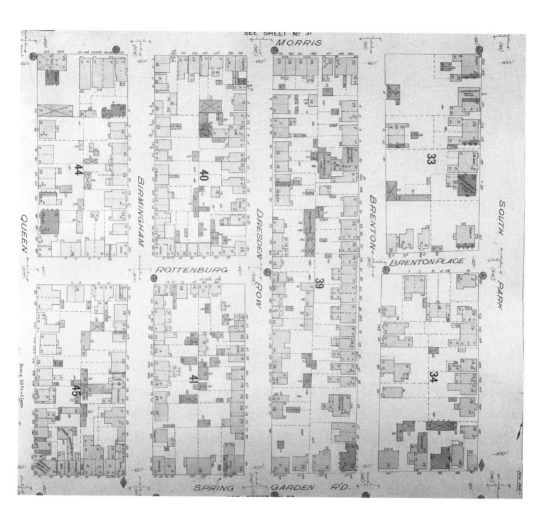

**1911 FIRE
INSURANCE MAP,
SCHMIDTVILLE**

By 1911 there was a considerable change in Schmidtville. The Halifax Grammar School was long gone to the edge of Citadel Hill, and O'Brien's Carriage Works on Brenton was now Adam McNutt's. At the interior corners of Schmidtville, there were numerous grocery stores, often operated by widows or unmarried women. A Mrs. James operated a private school on Brenton, and there were now a couple of Chinese laundries on Birmingham. Stephen Pettipas made shoes at 51 Birmingham and Hopgood Grocery Store's barn was at 53. Two dressmakers also lived on the street. Major Stephen sold liquor at 68 Dresden, as did James White, at 8 1/2 Rottenburg.

Some Schmidtville children probably went to Morris Street School or to Saint Mary's, a block and a half away on Pleasant. Few probably got a post-secondary education, although some influence of the Grammar School might have existed. The number of churches in the area had not changed since 1911. From the east, Saint Mary's Cathedral still towered over Schmidtville. St. Luke's Anglican Cathedral on Morris, which burned in 1905, was replaced by All Saints Cathedral on Tower Road to the southwest of Schmidtville.

For some, the German street names in Schmidtville became a problem, especially during the First World War. Therefore, in 1915 politicians proposed changing certain street names to less "offensive" ones. There would be no Coburg Road, no Brunswick Street, no Gottingen, no Dresden Row, and certainly no Rottenburg. Locally, nothing came of the proposal, but the next year Berlin, Ontario, became Kitchener. Then, in December 1917, the proposal to Anglicize Germanic street names reappeared. Four days after the Halifax Explosion, amid the hysteria, the *Herald* announced that "practically all Germans" would be arrested. In the 1950s, though, Rottenburg was changed to Clyde.

Due to the commercialization of Spring Garden Road, today about half of the original Schmidtville is gone. Nevertheless, most of the houses below Clyde Street are still used as residences, including a number of run-down rooming houses on Morris Street.

Chapter 3

Spring Garden Road

HUGH MILLS OF MILLS BROTHERS

At 235 acres, the South Common was the largest part of the Halifax Commons, land originally set aside for common pasturage and firewood. But a major problem facing governments in early Halifax was that too much of the town's lands were tax free, since a good portion of the land was military property, and thus tax-exempt. A very significant portion of the peninsula—including Point Pleasant Park, the Citadel, Fort Massey, and Fort Needham—paid no taxes.

The Commons, which were set out by surveyor Charles Morris in 1760, were a virtual wasteland. There were scrubby, scattered trees, swamp areas, and the Freshwater Stream that lazily meandered through it. The Common was described as "useless…dreary and barren." The town saw the development of the land as a way to collect more taxes for necessary improvements. Initially there were attempts to have private enterprise develop the South Common. As early as 1818 lots on upper Spring Garden Rood were granted, and government money was soon also invested for the area's development. After the city's incorporation in 1841, the development of Spring Garden Road, which ran directly through the centre of the South Common, was the focus of development. Only small pockets of open space like Victoria Park, the Public Gardens, and the Wanderers Grounds, serve as a reminder of the grand South Common's slow disappearance.

Spring Garden Road, the beginning of the Windsor Road, came to be the most fashionable area in the city. As it commercialized, the street reclaimed those South Enders who used to shop on Barrington and Gottingen Streets. South End business has become largely concentrated in the Spring Garden Road area over the last eighty years, with some auxiliary action on Barrington and Hollis. It wasn't always that way. Business started on Water Street, later spreading to Hollis and Barrington. Only late in the nineteenth century did Spring Garden Road start to become a major player. Since the 1920s, Spring Garden Road has dominated the high-end business in the South End.

In 1761 when the hatchet was buried in the Governor's Garden, the street was just a rough path from Pleasant Street toward the Freshwater Stream at what is now South Park Street. One branch led northwest to the Windsor, or "Great West," Road, and the other led south to Fort Massey. There was nothing on Spring Garden but the gambrel-roofed Poor House west of the modern library, and immediately to its east, a graveyard (now Grafton Park). By the time Spring Garden finally developed, it was the late 1820s. On the north side, past the almost finished Saint Mary's Cathedral and its old glebe, there was the Bridewell, or House of Correction, in what had been the Poor House. A new Poor House that had been erected before 1820 was behind it near the later Doyle Street. It would be replaced in 1869 by the South Street Poor House, the site of one of the greatest tragedies in the city's history.

**BROOKSIDE,
c.1935**

John Stayner's 1818 home, later called "Brookside," stood at Pyke's Bridge on the Freshwater Stream at South Park Street. Across the water, just west of the modern entrance of the Public Gardens, was Sergeant John George Pyke's home. Pyke was the chief police magistrate. When the Bridewell was established in 1815, he and two others were appointed magistrates, three constables were hired, and a man was hired to escort prisoners to and from the workhouse and inflict exactly thirty-nine lashes on juvenile offenders. This was the beginning of municipal government, the first gasp of civil rule in a town that was at the mercy of undisciplined soldiery and lieutenant governors who too often were military officers quick to pardon the military for its crimes.

When Spring Garden Road did develop, it gentrified. By the mid-nineteenth century, city directories were describing Spring Gardens as a "most delightful district devoted principally to private residences, all of which denote the comfortable circumstances of the occupants; while those of the more wealthy, surrounded by delightful grounds and shrubberies exhibit an elegance seldom met with in the lower provinces." One of the important factors in continuing the development of Spring Garden was the extension of the horse railway from Pleasant Street in 1867. An extra horse was used to get up the steep hill at Pleasant Street.

GRAFTON STREET METHODIST CHURCH, 1860

By the late 1800s, there were two new churches on Spring Garden: the Grafton Street Methodist and First Baptist. Grafton Street Methodist had been built in wood on the hillock in 1852, and with its square tower, resembled Saint Mary's. Sixteen years later, on February 25, 1868, it burned. Fortunately, the buildings on Grafton, including Saint Mary's College, were saved, as the strong wind carried the flames over them. The Methodists rebuilt it as a steeple-less stone church for thirty-six thousand dollars, but the church became Saint David's Presbyterian after its Methodists joined the United Church in 1925.

FIRST BAPTIST CHURCH FIRE, 1942

The 1887 First Baptist Church at Queen and Spring Garden was an offshoot of an earlier dispute concerning the ministerial succession at Saint Paul's and general dissatisfaction with the too-Catholic liturgy. The church was originally a small stone chapel on Granville, but after building its church hall at Queen Street, the congregation built their new church on Spring Garden and Queen.

Residences on Spring Garden Street were mixed while most of the street's stores were to the west. The well-known conservative letter writer, MPP, and House Speaker Judge John Marshall lived two houses short of Birmingham. Half a block west was Nicholas Sarre's home. Sarre had a barber shop on Hollis and his sons, James Jackson and Edge, were backers of the sculler George Brown, who died in 1875 before he could re-challenge for the world championship. Across Dresden at the corner was Kendrick's Grocery Store. Further west larger homes appeared. Daniel Cronan's estate with "Brier Cottage" and the adjacent double residence of Michael Dwyer, "Brookside," were near Pyke's Bridge. Cronan was a West Indian trader, while Dwyer was a senior official of the Tobin Tea Company.

THE VICTORIAN PUBLIC GARDENS LOOKING SOUTH, c.1879

Across the Freshwater Stream at South Park Street were the Horticultural Gardens, founded in 1836 and surrounded by a picket fence at least eight feet high. It was, however, less than half as deep as its successor, the Public Gardens, not even extending to Griffin's Pond (the Duck Pond), although this may have been because the undeveloped area near the pond was described as a "receptacle for dead cats, broken bottles, old boots, [and] worn out brooms."

The Public Gardens, South Park Street Gate, c.1889

The gardens society had taken a 999-year lease "in the western suburbs of Halifax." There was an admission cost, but the gardens were open to the public only one day per week. Featured were an archery range facing Summer Street and a skating rink near South Park. This rink, built in 1863, was the first covered rink in Canada and was also rented to the school board for the yearly public school examinations, being one of the few large halls available at that season. The rink lasted until 1889 when a larger rink, the Exhibition Building, was planned for Tower Road. The Horticultural Gardens also featured flower beds and a fountain. However, by 1874 the Horticultural Gardens were in debt and sold out to the city for fifteen thousand dollars. The property was combined with the city garden to the north, including Griffin's Pond, and became the sixteen-acre Public Gardens.

HALIFAX CITY COUNCIL.
1913

RICHARD POWER, 1913

Power is at the right end of the third row from the top in this photo taken in 1913. Three of the first superintendents of the Public Gardens were members of the Power family. The longest-serving superintendent was Richard Power, an Irishman born in 1841 in Lismore, County Waterford. Power served his apprenticeship in England and America, and was appointed superintendent in May 1872. By October, he and his wife were residents of the lunatic asylum. According to the *Acadian Recorder* of October 23, 1872, Mrs. Nick Shea, the widow of the last caretaker of the Horticultural Gardens, took advantage of the Powers' suspicious natures in this "exceedingly lonely location next to the cemetery and a considerable distance from other residents." She heaped abuse on the Powers for replacing her husband, a rough character who had been "a terror to the Commons." Power imagined he saw Shea's ghost wandering about carrying a stick, accompanied by a dog.

SUPERINTENDENT'S COTTAGE, PUBLIC GARDENS, N.D.

Miraculously for the age, Power recovered. His recovery was so complete that in 1884, he was presented with a purse of gold by Halifax citizens. He used the money to travel to Great Britain and Ireland doing research for the Public Gardens and the city landscapes. Toward the end of his life, tragedy struck again in the careless death of his successor and son, Richard Jr., in alighting from a moving car in 1921. The old man, who had retired in 1917, came back for a few years as superintendent. After his death in 1934, his grandson George took over. Three generations of Powers had lived at the superintendent's cottage at the corner of Sackville Street and Bell Road.

To the north of the Public Gardens were the Wanderers Grounds. Organized as an athletic club in 1882, the Wanderers Club received its present location at nominal rent from the city in 1886, and the first clubhouse opened in 1890. The club was known for its epic rugby struggles with both Dalhousie and the Navy, but the Wanderers Grounds were also used for cricket, lawn bowling, boxing, and hockey. In 1897 Starr Manufacturing offered its beautiful cup for the winner of the local hockey championship. The Wanderers beat the perennial champs, the Dartmouth Chebuctos, 3–1 to take the cup on their first try.

During World War Two, the Wanderers Grounds were taken over by the Navy League, who established both wet and dry canteens for Allies on leave. After the war, the club, despite concessions from the city, was failing. In 1958 the city took over the grounds and wrote off the club's tax bill. The Wanderers Grounds had gone the way of the Horticultural Gardens. Still, the grounds were used for city sports, and one of the club's original activities, lawn bowing, continued.

Two blocks north of the Public Gardens, at Carlton near the Camp Hill Cemetery, was Spring Garden Academy, a school run by Rev. James Woods. Beginning in January 1856, Woods had taught at Dalhousie College High School, where he was assistant to the principal, Hugo Reid. An irresolvable quarrel arose and Woods, who acted as principal while Reid was away, resigned, setting up his own school in competition. The school had about an acre of land, a residence, and a gym. The dispute between the two men led to the closure of poor Dalhousie—again.

At Spring Garden Academy, Woods claimed to be training his students in physical and intellectual health. A French master was available, as was training in art, something at which Woods excelled. On the other hand, he was no progressive educator. Getting other students to help hold an offender, he would have them quote Shakespeare as he administered the three-inch-wide strap to any transgressors.

**MARGARET
MARSHALL
SAUNDERS,
C.1922**

On the southwest corner of Carleton Street and Spring Garden was
a large brown home built by J. W. Rhuland for Rev. E. M. Saunders,
author and pastor of the Granville Street Baptist Church. His daughter,
Margaret Marshall Saunders, was an author who used the pen name
Marshall Saunders in her early writing career. Educated in Europe, in
1892 Margaret (1861–1947) wrote *Beautiful Joe*. By the 1930s, it had
sold seven million copies and been translated into fourteen languages.

THE OLD CONVENT OF THE SACRED HEART, C.1872

The dominating Convent of the Sacred Heart was across Summer Street. It had a crenellated (castle-like) border around the roof and a similar tower on its Summer Street chapel. The property was surrounded by a low, open wooden fence. There was a well-known public pump outside the fence on Spring Garden, and willows graced the area. Next to the chapel was the Summer Street School, originally a barn. It was operated for the poor by the convent.

JUDGE SAMUEL L.
SHANNON, C.1885

Continuing east on Spring Garden was Judge Samuel Shannon's house, built by his father James in 1852 as a cottage. Samuel and his wife, Ann Fellows, moved next door in 1872, building a high stucco house at the current site of the Bank of Nova Scotia. Shannon was a distinguished graduate of King's College, despite being a Methodist. He was also a member of Dalhousie's Board of Governors and a Conservative member of the local legislature. He was also a supporter of Confederation. Shannon was well known for defending Dalhousie against attempts to dissolve it in 1864. It seems Acadia had not forgiven Dalhousie for not hiring the Baptist professor Edmund Crawley more than a generation before.

Further east, W. A. Shank's legendary soda shop was at the southwest corner of Spring Garden and Dresden Row. An old-fashioned soda fountain, it did not have a long marble counter but a short one near the door, with metal-rimmed wells for bottles of various flavours. Also, there was a glass globe with a figure inside, which water flowed through. Shank gave many their first taste of soda or ginger beer.

MAGISTRATE HENRY PRYOR, N.D.

On the other side of Birmingham and set back twenty-five feet was the residence of Henry Pryor, magistrate and mayor in the late 1840s and again in the 1850s. The city's first stipendiary magistrate, he took care of minor and preliminary cases. Henry was orphaned at twelve, but graduated from the Grammar School and King's College.

BELLEVUE HOUSE, 1919

Across Queen Street, Bellevue House, used for many years as the local general's residence, dominated the next block. It was three storeys tall and had two chimneys and several large windows. The building, which was used as a hospital during the Halifax Explosion, lasted until 1955, when it was declared surplus.

GENERAL SIR CHARLES HASTINGS DOYLE, c.1864

From Bellevue, General Charles Hastings Doyle, the local military commander, went to Point Pleasant Park in 1865. He sat in his saddle for five days during the Fenian Threats directing the cutting of trees so the Citadel guns could be ranged properly. He was knighted for his efforts against the fanatical Irishmen.

Closely associated with Bellevue was the tragic Adele Hugo (1830–1915), daughter of Victor Hugo, the famous French author. Strongly affected by the drowning of her sister, Adele then irrationally pursued Albert Pinson, a young army officer, from England to Halifax. She was frequently seen waiting outside Bellevue in the 1860s and eventually followed Pinson to Barbados, where she broke down completely. She was returned to Paris and committed for the rest of her life to an asylum. Her father was a faithful visitor.

The new eleven-thousand-pound County Courthouse appeared between Bellevue's drill shed and Saint Paul's cemetery. Construction got off to a bad start when the original contractor quit, so George Laing, who had also carved the lion on top of the Welsford–Parker Monument, took over. The Courthouse was designed by C. P. Thomas of Toronto, and completed in 1859 with a big cupola. Additional wings were added in the late-nineteenth and twentieth centuries.

ST. MARY'S
CATHEDRAL
AND ST. PAUL'S
CEMETERY, N.D.

After St. Peter's Church was rebuilt and opened in 1829, it was renamed St. Mary's. It sufficed for many years as the major Catholic church in Halifax. But by 1860, Archbishop Thomas Connolly felt there should be a more impressive church in a society riven by religious and political differences. The new church was to be "a credit to religion, an ornament to the city, and a monument to tell future generations of the zeal of the Catholic people…" He organized a campaign to lengthen the front of the church and to add a towering spire. By 1875, with the cathedral virtually completed, Connolly died. His successor finished it.

PARKER–
WELSFORD
MONUMENT,
SAINT PAUL'S
CEMETERY, 1860

Shown in the background of the monument photo above are the long ago removed cupola on the courthouse. The monument in Saint Paul's graveyard commemorates the Crimean War heroes Captain William Parker and Major Augustus Welsford. The photo was taken at the monument's unveiling on July 17, 1860, and is one of the earliest examples of outdoor photography taken in Halifax.

SPRING GARDEN ROAD AT QUEEN LOOKING WEST, 1893

The commercialization of Spring Garden Road transformed the area. In 1890 the *Herald* described the development of business on Spring Garden Road, saying it had been transformed from "ancient line of edifices into modernized places of businesses and residences." Gone were the days when everything was downtown and there were only two shops, Urquhart's and Kendrick's, on Spring Garden. Bellevue House had its grounds beautified, while the First Baptist Church occupied the garden of the old Poor House, near the site of Robertson's Livery Stable on Doyle Street.

As a youngster, famous South End resident Francis Fitzgerald used to drive the teams to Robertson's Livery. Born on Brenton Street in 1869, Fitzgerald later served in the South African War against the Boers. He also commanded the new post on Herschel Island in the high Arctic to demonstrate Canadian sovereignty and was chosen to attend the London coronation of King George V in 1910. Fitzgerald's end came when, as a member of the Royal Northwest Mounted Police, he took a chance that he could get the winter mail to Dawson, Yukon, travelling light and without native guides. He and his men became lost and died of starvation.

MILLS BROTHERS CHRISTMAS DISPLAY, 1948

Strangely, the major commercial development of the next two blocks of Spring Garden stalled for about sixty years until the 1950s. Delayed by the First World War, the post-war recession, the Great Depression, and World War Two, the only significant commercial enterprises that appeared were Nielsen's and Mills Dry Goods and Ladies Wear, the Lord Nelson Hotel nine years later in 1928, Hubley's Imperial Oil Station at Dresden and Spring Garden, and the Dominion Store at the old Cronan estate in 1931.

Hugh Mills from Lockport became a partner in Nielsen and Mills, a 1919 dry-goods store on Spring Garden. Nielsen left and in 1928 Hugh's younger brother, Willett, joined and the store changed its name to Mills Bros. Targeting upper-middle-class ladies, the store expanded from fabrics and threads to suits and hats. Mills had another, more public, career as "Uncle Mel," a well-remembered radio personality and was one of the organizers of the Theatre Arts Guild in 1931.

THE LORD NELSON HOTEL, 1941

A first-class hotel was a long-time dream of Spring Garden Road. The Lord Nelson was born during Halifax's brief acquaintance with "Roaring Twenties" after its organizers were able to raise $1,240,000. Opened August 30, 1928, the hotel struggled through the 1930s but eventually made money.

It was the 1950s before the blocks to South Park were commercialized. First, the Bank of Nova Scotia destroyed Shannon's fine home at Brenton and Spring Garden for new offices. In 1958, on the north side next to Alderman Hamilton's brick terrace, appeared the reinforced concrete building housing Nova Scotia Trust. Diagonally across the street, one block west, the four-floor Sovereign Building was built in 1955. Traffic lights appeared in 1959 and CIBC demolished the rundown Quirk home at the northwest corner of Dresden and Spring Garden to build their new business. Much of the housing between Clyde Street and Spring Garden, including half of Schmidtville, was levelled for the convenience of shoppers.

The Sacred Heart Convent became very popular with Catholic families to educate their girls for "proper" marriages, although by 1857–58 there were also many Protestant students. By 1905, nine years before Mount Saint Vincent University, the Convent also had its two-year post-secondary course recognized by Dalhousie, so graduates could enter the third year of a BA. The school was damaged in the Halifax Explosion but soon was able to help in relief efforts although the building had no heat. It took in American doctors and nurses and thirty orphans before its regular students returned in January 1918 to the still unheated building.

OLD CITY BUILDING AND MARKET, JULY 1886. THE HALIFAX CITIZENS' LIBRARY HAD BEEN IN THE CITY HALL TO THE LEFT.

Halifax's first real public library, the Citizens' Free Library, appeared in June 1864, with 1,400 volumes for 240 patrons. It was housed in the old City Building, near the Dartmouth ferry landing. Anyone eighteen years of age and older could borrow if sponsored by a taxpayer. Students could borrow if approved by their teachers, and visitors could borrow on a guarantee from a citizen member. Borrowing was limited to one book per day, and fines were two cents per day. The library featured men's and women's reading rooms. There were over six hundred subscribers by February 1865.

In August 1873, the library moved to 263 Barrington (Lockman Extension) across from the back of Salem Chapel. Sir William Young donated the 1830 Mechanics' Library on the condition that the city find a suitable site. The new library held six thousand volumes and Samuel Creed was the manager, making a theoretical five hundred dollars per year by 1876, although he had trouble collecting it. The city council was neglecting the library, and the collection became perennially starved for funds. Another move to Argyle Hall, diagonally across from Dalhousie, in June 1879-80 meant one large room. There were now twelve thousand volumes, but very few new ones, and with 1,500 books out for repair, readership declined further.

In an 1884 interview in the *Halifax Morning Herald*, Creed mentioned that he had to refuse one borrower until he stopped bringing back books smelling of a stable, and that he had set up a table in a corner to glue books back together. He noted that the year before he had repaired one thousand books and was spending as much time with the paste pot as with the pen.

HALIFAX MEMORIAL LIBRARY, C.1950

In 1892 the city moved the library to the attic of its new City Hall. In this bright, spacious area, conditions improved. By 1895 the Citizens' Library had twenty-two thousand volumes, making it the second-largest collection in the city, and the only free one. An attempt was made in 1901 to have a combined library, art school, and art gallery, with outside funding. Andrew Carnegie, a major American capitalist, had offered Sydney fifteen thousand dollars, Saint John fifty thousand dollars, and Halifax seventy-five thousand dollars. All Halifax had to do was guarantee maintenance of the building and the collection—a total of seven thousand dollars per year. The city debated ad nauseam whether the building would be located at Victoria Park, the unused south end of Saint Paul's graveyard, or Grafton Park. The opportunity was frittered away, with the city simply not willing to make a financial commitment. Halifax would not get a sufficient library until the Halifax Memorial Library was open at Grafton Park on November 12, 1951.

COBURG APARTMENTS, 1919.

In the early twentieth century, the upper part of Spring Garden began to sprout apartments, joining a number of fine houses including Havelock Hart's eight-thousand-dollar home built in 1898 on Summer. Coburg Apartments appeared at Robie and Spring Garden in 1919, but Garden Crest, Halifax's first luxury apartments, had appeared five years earlier on Summer, opposite the Public Gardens. Unfortunately, the commercialization of Spring Garden also brought crime. In 1929 Halifax was shocked to find that one of Alderman Hamilton's fine Victorian brick residences was not only illegally selling liquor, but also women. Seven years earlier, on November 1, 1922, L. A. Corkham, owner of Corkham's Drug Store at 160 Spring Garden, was fatally shot there. No one was convicted.

Halifax, especially between 1770 and 1890, was considered, along with Montreal and Quebec, one of the best theatrical and musical cities in British North America. As early as 1768, there were actors performing in Halifax who had appeared at Drury Lane and Covent Garden in London. Halifax even saw what may have been the first Canadian play in English—*Acadius: or, Love in a Calm*, a 1774 comedy. In the early 1800s the tiny Halifax Amateur Theatre became the city's first semi-permanent theatre.

The next South End theatre was the Spring Garden Road Theatre, which held its first performance in June 1847. American touring companies and local military troupes entertained audiences through the early years of the theatre, but it wasn't until American E. A. Southern renovated the old barn in 1857 that the theatre began to thrive. Southern put in gas lighting and a large stage. He also jammed in nine hundred seats, almost doubling the capacity, but crowding the stage. To religious conservatives, Southern was an enemy, if not the Devil incarnate. The *Presbyterian Witness* was inventive in its diatribes: "In the old days we had the Pope, the Devil and the Spaniard, now we have the Pope, the Devil and E. A. Southern." In 1859, his last year in Halifax, Southern presented several well-known pieces including *Lucretia Borgia* and *She Stoops to Conquer*. The famous American actress Matilda Heron also appeared as Medea, the Greek enchantress, and her final Halifax performance was considered one of the greatest ever. The Spring Garden Road Theatre slowly died without Southern, struggling through the 1860s with comedies and occasionally Shakespearean plays. Southern later became famous with the creation of the character Lord Dundreary.

After several false starts, and great skepticism, the Academy of Music—the South End's third significant theatre—finally opened on January 9, 1877, at the east end of Spring Garden at Pleasant. Audiences varied with the Academy's shows. The upper balcony usually included several groups of the less affluent. Among these were young mothers and their children, well-dressed schoolboys, young Romeos and Juliets, soldiers on leave, delegates from "Afric's sunny climes," and a few seedy characters. The better off were below and, in general, the audience tended to sensationalism. Oscar Wilde appearance in 1882 was one of the Academy's highlights.

Designed by the English architect A. M. Jackson, the Academy of Music was magnificent. Built of brick-covered stucco, it was 90 feet wide on Pleasant Street, but 125 feet deep. There were three double doors at the entrance, with the ticket office on the right. Swinging doors, covered with green leather, led to the orchestra and parquet (main floor) below the dress circle. The parquet seats were separated from the orchestra pit by a white and gold railing. The dress circle had patent swing seats of scarlet and was reached by broad stairs from the vestibule. The sloping floors were carpeted and the audience of 1,500 had a good view. Above the dress circle was the upper gallery that did not project much over the dress circle. The ceiling was frescoed. Near the front was a portrait of Shakespeare on one side and either Chaucer or Aristotle on the other (the reporter was not sure). Between were the words, "Comedy, Poetry, Tragedy. Lecture, Music and Opera." One of the first electrically lighted buildings, it was dominated by the big chandelier which wowed the audience when suddenly illuminated. The stage, with its large rotating section, was a minor wonder.

Opening night featured the Rudolphson Quartette and the Boston Philharmonic Club supporting the Halifax Philharmonic Union. Prices were the highest yet: $1.50 for reserved seats and 50 cents for the upper galleries. Still, the place was packed and the audience seemed satisfied. For the first few years the theatre did quite well, generally filling the hall, although the return on the investment was not large. It soon became obvious, however, that a town of forty thousand was not large enough to support nightly performances. Despite showing matinees for housewives, the arrival of the horse-drawn trams on Spring Garden Road, and the running of a late ferry to Dartmouth, the Academy would not become more financially secure until Halifax and Dartmouth grew.

In 1914 the Academy showed its first movie. Four years later the theatre became a movie house and renamed the Majestic. In June 1929, "after years of shabby gentility," the former Academy of Music went down fighting under the assault of wreckers. The last show was Victor Herbert's *Fortune Teller*.

CAPITOL THEATRE, 1932

By the late 1920s, Famous Players had constructed a series of 150 movie houses across North America. The Capitol, on the site of the Academy of Music, was the last and one of the grandest. The theme of the 2,014-seat theatre was Medieval/Elizabethan. An armoured knight guarded the drawbridge which led into the theatre. There were plush red seats arranged on two levels. The balcony no longer held the "gods," but the loges, or best seats near the front.

On the pseudo-stone walls were armorial shields and above all, the historical paintings of Emanuel Briffo, the theatre artist for Famous Players. These included the "Founding of Halifax," the "Shannon and Chesapeake," and "Wolfe Landing at Louisbourg." The ceiling had the obligatory chandeliers. The Capitol was thirty percent bigger than the Academy for a population that had doubled to almost eighty thousand. Opening night, October 31, 1930, with the rising contralto Portia White, sold out in two hours. Shows were "popularly priced," and continuous from 2 p.m. Movie matinees were thirty-five cents for adults, fifteen cents for children. In the evening adults paid fifty-five cents, kids twenty-five.

PORTIA WHITE,
N.D.

The first night's receipts went to the Goodfellow's Club, while the provincial government rescinded the theatre tax. The Capitol had arrived just in time for the Great Depression. Besides Goodfellow's, the Commercial Club also had charity shows. But an offer of free admission with canned food on December 16, 1938, yielded 1,700 items.

The theatre, however, had some trouble filling the spaces between movie runs. In the fall of 1933 there was too much vaudeville, a genre which was going out of fashion. The Capitol finally settled on musical nights, often with Jerry Naugler's orchestra, a regular feature from late 1934 to the summer of 1935. On November 26, 1934, Naugler featured those cute kids with the evocative name, the "Tinymites." Even during the Depression the Capitol brought in some fine musicians. Portia White sang again on March 15, 1931, this time for the Home for Coloured Children. Mischa Elman played his violin to a thrilled house on April 20, 1932. Nine months later, Nicola Orloff performed for the Community Concert Association.

The theatre had a strong role to play leading up to, and during, World War Two. On October 1, 1935, Dr. T. Z. Koo spoke at the theatre on Japan's "Efforts on Behalf of World Peace." In late September 1938, the theatre broadcast Chamberlain's speech on Czechoslovakia, "Peace with honour." In the fall of 1941 the theatre was collecting aluminum under the motto of "Throw a Pot at Hitler," sponsored by the Red Cross. On December 20, 1941, the evening concert was for the Queen's Canadian Fund and aid to beleaguered Russia. In the ensuing war years the theatre also collected fat, which was used to make glycerine, a component of the explosive nitroglycerine. In October 1943, the theatre began cancelling Sunday night shows to save power.

SAILORS PASS BY THE CAPITOL THEATRE DURING THE VE DAY RIOT, 1945

Halifax's VE Day Riot closed the Capitol for five days. The riots lasted for two days and resulted in three deaths and saw the widespread looting of businesses—particularly liquor stores.

Despite brief attempts to re-invent itself, the Capitol's decline was swift in the new age of television. In 1974 the theatre was torn down by Maritime Tel and Tel for its office building. The single screen, no matter how grand, was dead. The first theatres of the South End are gone, but their spirit lives on in Neptune Theatre and Dalhousie's Rebecca Cohn Theatre.

Chapter 4

The Old South End

SOUTH PARK STREET, C.1900

O ne of the most noticeable things about the Old South End are all the big Victorian mansions in the Tower Road and South Park Street area. There are dozens of wooden houses of various colours and in various styles. They often have Italianate storm porches, especially on Tower Road. The Old South End, whose core is between South, Tower, Inglis, and Barrington, was predominately upper-middle class. Its residents, who Raddall described with considerable literary licence as Halifax's equivalent of Boston's Back Bay Brahmans, were "urbane, well educated, generous…but prone to haggle over ten cents" and only found "contentment behind…their bulky, brick or brownstone fronts."

FORSHAW DAY'S PAINTING OF THE FRESHWATER STREAM, 1858

Dominating the Old South End was the Freshwater Stream. Originating just beyond the North Common in a swamp near St. Matthias' Church, the Freshwater Stream drifted southeast. It filled the Egg Pond, flowed into the Public Gardens where it formed Griffin's Pond (the "duck pond"), before running down the west side of South Park Street. The stream crossed above South Street and flowed through the edge of Holy Cross Cemetery before plunging down a ten-metre waterfall, which powered Henry Artz's tannery. Heading southeast, it entered the harbour at the corner of Pleasant and Inglis Streets, where a nearby industrial area needed a plentiful supply of water.

By the mid-nineteenth century, the Freshwater Stream was becoming more and more affected by the city's growth. It had been made to strictly conform to South Park Street's west side and, in 1843, Holy Cross Cemetery opened, diverting the stream past the graves. Even worse, the pristine stream was turning into a major sewer. By October 20, 1874, it had been forced into a culvert at Freshwater Park (near the corner of Pleasant and Inglis), removing the stink and allowing the area to be divided into building lots. At least twice, this terribly insulted brook got its revenge. On March 17, 1953, the stream undermined Fenwick Street, causing an oil truck to fall five metres below. Cellars also flooded on Fenwick and South. Dynamite was eventually used to clear the morass. Today, all that is left of the stream is the duck pond in the Public Gardens, the babbling, badly polluted stream draining it, and the unmarked, much-reduced Freshwater Park at Inglis and Barrington.

The Trider House and the Kissing Bridge, c.1870

At the foot of Inglis Street and Pleasant Street was the so-called "Kissing Bridge." The original wooden bridge was once part of the fashionable Mall from Saint Paul's Church. Inglis started just beyond the Kissing Bridge where Pleasant Street forked, one branch (Pleasant) continuing south along the shore to Point Pleasant Park, the other climbing toward Tower Road. About 1825, just up from the Kissing Bridge, John Trider built his three-floor stone building for transient British officers. In 1957, it was torn down for a service station.

The Old South End originated from three major properties. The first was the already described Murphy's/Fitzgerald's farm on Massey Hill, the second the Smith brothers' farm and tannery on the other side of the Freshwater Steam, and the third the Tremaine property on the south side of Inglis Street back to Atlantic Street. In 1812, the Smiths received a block bounded by South Street, Tower Road, Inglis Street, and South Park Street. Later, they extended their property to the east, reaching the Freshwater Stream. One of the conditions of that sale was that the public and their cattle would have free access to the stream. The property now bridged the area between Jimmy Fitzgerald's former farm on Fort Massey Hill and Major Bazelgette's land at Inglis and Tower. In the 1820s the Smiths created a sensation when one of them was found headless in a tannery vat. Apparently, he had had too much schnapps and tumbled in head-first.

When the last of the Smiths died in 1861, their sixty-acre property was divided and sold. The sell-off began at their tannery at Queen and Green on July 4, 1862. In three days, hundreds of lots, which had significant frontage on the street, were disposed of. This was the greatest sell-off since Jimmy Fitzgerald's fifty acres on Fort Massey Hill two generations before. The Smith sell-off led to the development of the north side of Inglis Street, but it would be about 1900 before all the Smith lots were taken.

More than anyone, the Tremaines were responsible for the development of the south side of Inglis Street. Jonathan Tremaine, a Loyalist, had fled to Nova Scotia in 1785. He bought fifty acres on what is now the south side of Inglis stretching from South Bland almost to Tower Road and down to where Atlantic Street would later be. Tremaine built a ropewalk—a shed for winding fibres into a rope—on the west side of South Bland. It extended almost all the way down to Atlantic Street. In his will, he divided his land into eleven large lots, eight of which went to his children. His son John took over the ropewalk, and in 1822 built a fine house worth one thousand pounds. This was a mistake for four years earlier Nova Scotia had declared its ports free. Tremaine saw his business threatened by Americans who could produce rope on a large scale. An appeal to the legislature did no good, and he began to go into debt to Enos Collins. Tremaine eventually defaulted on his mortgage and Collins got the property. Ruined, John Tremaine left the city in 1837.

THORNDEAN, 1930   Thorndean, with massive end chimneys and an Italianate storm porch, has a wall that is hard against the sidewalk. Its most infamous resident was James Forman, who stole $314,976.68 from the Bank of Nova Scotia. Originally a small wine merchant on Water Street, he was appointed cashier of the bank on its formation in 1832. Forman had bought the block bounded by Inglis, Lucknow, South Park, and Fenwick from the Smiths. Forman had skimmed the bank's accounts for a quarter of a century, enabling he and his apparently innocent wife to live a life of high society. After handing over his properties, he fled to New York, then to London, without his wife. He died there in 1871 at seventy-five before he could be extradited.

THE OLD SOUTH END FROM BELLEVUE HOUSE, SHOWING SAINT LUKE'S CATHEDRAL, 1872

Saint Luke's Anglican Cathedral at Church Street and Morris was a symbol of exclusivity. It was opened on May 14, 1848, by Rev. William Cogswell as a mere "chapel of ease" for old Saint Paul's Church. This made it the first church in the Old South End area. By 1858 it had become a parish in its own right. A brick schoolhouse became their Sunday school in 1862. Saint Luke's later developed two "chapels of ease" of its own—Saint Stephen's at Coburg and Robie, and Saint Alban's on upper Tower Road. Plans were made for a proper cathedral and in August 1887, the cornerstone was laid on a piece of land donated by Judge Bliss at Robie and Coburg, then a rather remote area. But just as construction was to start, Bishop Binney died unexpectedly, and the project stalled. Two years later, construction was revived when the possibility of using granite from the abandoned provincial penitentiary in Francklyn Park came about. But this fell through, too. It was only the burning of St. Luke's in December 1905 that led to the revival of the idea. This led to All Saints Cathedral on Morris Street and Tower Road in 1910. Thirty-one years later, Saint Luke's old parish hall became St. George's Orthodox Church.

HOLY CROSS
CEMETERY, OUR
LADY OF SORROWS
CHAPEL, SOUTH
PARK STREET,
1928

Our Lady of Dolores (Sorrows) Chapel was built in a day. But the grounds and basement were prepared several weeks before. The most prominent burial at the Holy Cross Cemetery is Sir John Thompson, Prime Minister of Canada from 1892–94. A convert from Methodism, he died within an hour of being honoured by Queen Victoria on December 12, 1894. Thompson was only forty-eight. When he left only twenty thousand dollars to his family, including a mentally challenged daughter, a subscription was taken up. The cemetery also is the final resting place for several of Halifax's prominent bishops, buried in a row at the top of the hill.

Not far from Our Lady of Sorrows was Morris Street School, one of the best in the city that served many children of the elite. The school was finished in 1868 "on an elevated and central site" at a cost of $27,483. The school had an outstanding staff, and one staff member, Principal John Jack, also taught mathematics at the short-lived Technological Institute based at Dalhousie College. At $1,350 per year he was the best-paid teacher in the city. Tragically, he lost everything when he came into the school drunk in the spring of 1878, assaulted his popular vice-principal, Miss MacCullogh, and insulted trustee Sam Brookfield. The school's parents demanded his dismissal, city council agonized, ultimately dismissing him and rejecting his appeals. Jack then established

Fort Massey Academy, a private school, but it quickly failed. Jack sold everything in December 1879, and left for England, disappearing from history. Morris Street School expanded in 1884 but did not survive a falling student population in the twentieth century. It was demolished in 1951.

The second church in the Old South End, St. Andrew's, opened in May 1871 at Tobin and Pleasant. Saint Andrew's was Gothic but had a controversial organ, introduced in the old church in 1867. Organs, or any instrumental music, was said to be "altogether alien to the spirit and usage of Scotland, and also Nova Scotia." Perhaps the real reason was that some thought an organ was too Catholic, but then so too was the Gothic style.

FORT MASSEY PRESBYTERIAN CHURCH, QUEEN AND TOBIN, c.1895

Fort Massey Presbyterian, at the top of Tobin Street, was also a Gothic expression, this time in stone and brick. Financed by subscription, Fort Massey was opened the same year as Saint Andrew's.

On March 7, 1876, the *Morning Chronicle* reported that the new Fort Massey minister, Rev. Dr. Robert Burns, had invited the defrocked Catholic priest, Rev. Charles Chiniquy, to speak, despite the latter's well-known attacks on his former denomination. The inevitable riot followed, led by young Catholic hotheads. Chiniquy escaped with some difficulty due to Sheriff Garrett Cotter, who put his duty ahead of his Irish background. Cotter had a member of the congregation, George Buist, who resembled the ex-priest, go out the side door on Tobin, escorted by two police officers. The mob chased them. Meanwhile, he escorted the troublemaker out the front door and put him on the next train. The church suffered a number of broken windows and a congregation that was terrified when the mob stormed the front door. But, again, Chiniquy escaped the consequences of his provocation.

FORT MASSEY (THE ODELL HOUSE) AT TOBIN AND QUEEN, N.D.

Previous to World War Two, the Odell home made news for an auction starting August 22, 1938. There were "two centuries" of silverware, furniture, and cutlery, objects that had been "touched by Royal hands," a sure draw at the time. The death of the last of the Odells, Mary, daughter of Elizabeth Bliss and the Honourable William Hunter Odell, had set it off. Buyers from all over North America appeared, including "half the summer residents of Chester." Four thousand dollars was made in the first day. The house was demolished in 1972.

THE EXHIBITION BUILDING, C.1880

On the west side of Tower, between Morris and Spring Garden, stood the big Exhibition Building. Opened in 1879, it was a skating rink during the winter, replacing the decrepit rink in the Public Gardens. Then, in the summer, it held the provincial agricultural show. The Exhibition Building had a huge hexagonal tower, and its red-slate roof had dormers. It was gas-lit at night and sun-lit by huge floor-to-ceiling windows at day. There was a balcony allowing a fine view of the main floor, which measured 210 feet by 60 feet. Skating balls, where many would dress up in costume, were frequent. Early hockey was also seen here. On March 14, 1888, the Wanderers and Royal Blues played an exciting exhibition game. Not only did ordinary people dress-up or play hockey, but John L. Sullivan fought a bare-knuckle exhibition match at the rink also.

In 1896 the city planned a new Exhibition Building. They wanted Morris Street to continue through the old site as a boulevard toward Dalhousie, and imagined that ornate dwellings, set back from the street, would appear along it. Despite initial resistance from the residents, the city opened the new building at Willow Park in the city's North End in 1897.

BISHOP CLARENDON WORRELL, N.D.

The last great Victorian institution on Tower was actually Edwardian: All Saints Cathedral, which was built on the former Exhibition site. Clarendon Worrell had the new cathedral built on six Exhibition lots, cutting costs to the bone. The cathedral was finished for only $125,000, when it should have cost at least $270,000. Copper replaced lead, plaster replaced cut stone, rubble fill replaced masonry. The disaster opened September in 1910. All Saints stood incomplete for many years, a burden on the Anglicans with its collapsing walls, flooding basements, and leaking ceilings. After spending twice the original amount, the parishioners finally received a stable structure, but with little stained glass and no central tower, its crowning glory.

Near All Saints stood the School for the Blind (originally called the Asylum for the Blind) facing Morris, and between South Park and Tower.
Financed initially by William Murdoch's estate's five thousand pounds
in 1867, the funds were given on the condition that a matching grant
be raised within five years. This was almost lost through inertia and
the resistance against the expropriation of part of the South Common.
"The Committee for the Preservation of the Commons" eventually surrendered, rationalizing that "the site resolved upon is the least objec-
tionable chosen being a detached portion of the Common—not...of
sufficient area to be...much account for any public purpose."

The school, which cost fourteen thousand dollars, opened August
1, 1871, with four students and two teachers. Fees were $120 per year.
The first director was Frederick Fraser (1850–1925), the son of a Windsor, Nova Scotia, medical doctor. He served a half-century, starting in
1873. Fraser had graduated from the Perkins Institute for the Blind in
Boston after he started to lose his sight at age seven.

Fraser worked hard to improve his school. In 1881, for example, he spoke at the Academy of Music on the necessity of free education for the blind. Lieutenant-Governor Adams George Archibald was present and the address was rated as "memorable." Apparently it was, for the next year the students had free tuition after the municipalities and province agreed to split the cost. Then, in 1883, Fraser changed the school's name from the pejorative "Asylum" to the neutral "School." Braille books were also expensive, and by 1893, the school had only 170 volumes in its library. Five years later free postage was authorized for such books in Canada. Again, Fraser was instrumental. In 1913 Fraser received a vote of thanks from the House of Assembly for his forty years of service. He died a dozen years later. Today, the modern school on Gorsebrook Field is named after him.

Another Victorian institution, Tower Road School, was built in 1874. Originally a four-room wooden structure, it was designed to catch the overflow from the Morris Street School. Tower Road was still, at the time, beyond the built-up area of the South End, so not all families were likely to send their children there. As the old South End filled in, Tower Road School was rebuilt in brick in 1912. Among the better-known students were Hugh MacLellan, the novelist, and Rich Little, the comedian. Less known is the principal, Lt. George M. Sylvester, who, in 1914, caught up in the euphoria of defending the Empire, went to war. By 1916, he was just a memory.

The school's library only contained 189 books in 1905, just a few more than the Blind School a decade earlier. Also, Tower Road's courses included military drill, temperance speeches, and lectures on moral and patriotic duties. There was no gymnasium until 1955. Today, no longer a public school, Tower Road School is the Tower Road campus of the private Halifax Grammar School.

Tower Hamlets, at the upper part of Tower Road, was the precursor of Greenbank, the twentieth-century railway shantytown off Young Avenue. This was a rural area, with big estates between it and the edge of the city. The elite who lived here included Enos Collins, George Whidden, and the Cogswells. The villagers had two dozen or so small homes of which almost one-third were held by families with Irish names. Totally isolated, they were a kilometre from the edge of Halifax, and no horse-drawn street railway within two kilometres. There were, however, some opportunities for low-pay employment, which allowed such a marginal community to exist. Initially, the provincial penitentiary in Francklyn Park, if not offering free room and board for a set period, offered guard duty and kitchen work. Pine Hill Divinity College on Francklyn Street probably offered cleaning and kitchen jobs, the big estates had need of extra farm labour, and Point Pleasant Park also had a need for labourers.

A fire in December 1895 gives a view into the life of one Tower Hamlet family, the Delaneys. They had been in a two-storey house on Tower Road three years and already had two fires, which had "pretty well destroyed" the place. Mr. Delaney was a labourer, probably at Point Pleasant Park. Calling the fire department was not very efficient, since no one in the area had a telephone. Instead, a neighbour, "Mr. Burns in that little house," had the key to a call box on the Bower, a good hike down Tower Road. A short time after the call, the pumper, trailing a thick cloud of steam, was seen thundering up Tower pulled by several powerful horses. Someone, probably young John Delaney, directed them to the fire. He had lots of practice.

By the turn of the twentieth century the section of Inglis that reached to Tower was mostly filled. At the corner of South Bland and Inglis, Sam M. Brookfield built his home in 1892. Later an investment property, in 1942 it was sold to the Navy League as a Merchant Marine Officers Club. A year later the building received an addition and the bay windows were removed. In 1959, it became a tourist home, Winnie's Lodge.

GEORGE WRIGHT,
C.1885

Much of the Victorian streetscape along South Park Street was due to George Wright. In 1896 he built seven houses in several different styles on South Park while on Letson's Lane he built more modest, working-class homes. This became Wright Avenue with its houses adjacent to Holy Cross Cemetery. Then came Young Avenue, the South End's first exclusive street. After Pleasant Street started to fill, the elite had begun to move to the Brunswick Street area. Here lived such notables as the Cunards and Sandford Fleming. With Young Avenue, the South End could, for the first time, offer its own upper-class street.

Young Avenue, Halifax, N.S.

YOUNG AVENUE LOOKING NORTH, c.1920

The boulevarded southern end of South Park Street, Young Street, was developed by Sir William Young. Special legislation was passed in the Nova Scotia Legislature in 1896 to ensure that "any home had to be assessed at more than $2,000 if wood, or $3,000 in brick." Then, "no building could be erected within 180 ft (60 m) of Young Avenue without permission of the City Council and it was forbidden to use such buildings as a hotel, house of entertainment, boarding house, shop or for sale of liquor."

The street developed slowly, although the 1911 assessment shows the homes that were built were valuable, including the Alexander Hobrecker "Castle" worth twenty-five thousand dollars. Hobrecker was a Prussian who had won the Memorial Cross for his action in the Seven Weeks' War (1866) against Austria. He arrived in Nova Scotia in 1870, married Charlotte Clemen the next year, and was naturalized in 1877. Today his house is better known as the Oland Castle, or Lindola. The 1928 city directory shows Young Avenue still half-empty, with ten homes on the east side and sixteen on the west. By 1951 most lots were filled and more familiar names were appearing. Victor de Bedia Oland lived with Nancy and their family at number 88, for example. The Olands had added a garage and done other alterations in 1936–37, a hard time for most people.

The Old South End developed from the elite living on Pleasant Street. First, they climbed over Fort Massey Hill, then spilled across the Freshwater Stream, and finally spread south toward Point Pleasant Park. However they tried, there was not enough of the upper classes to fill it. Mere middle-class homes appeared on streets such as Victoria and Lucknow and the poor even established themselves on the edge of the wonderful park that would grace Young Avenue. So it remains.

Chapter 5

The Industrial South End

THE INDUSTRIAL SOUTH END BEFORE THE OCEAN TERMINALS, 1845

Today a dark slash, sutured by a number of bridges, cuts the greenness of the South End. Starting north of Quinpool Road and curving southeast, the slash finally runs east. East of Young Avenue, however, it becomes an open sore that separates the city from Point Pleasant Park. This is the railway cut that leads to the heart of the industrial South End, the Ocean Terminals, a contradiction to the South End's upper-class image.

Halifax has been a mostly ice-free port since its founding over 250 years ago. Sir John A. MacDonald even promoted Halifax as "Canada's winter port." Unfortunately, he awarded an important overseas mail contract to Allen Steamships of Montreal, which then used Portland, Maine, as its winter port, even after the Intercolonial Railway was completed to Halifax in 1876. The Intercolonial was soon losing five hundred thousand dollars a year, but managed to increase traffic to Halifax somewhat in the early 1880s, when the Deepwater Pier and grain elevator appeared. Still, without the mail contract, it could not make a profit and Portland remained, as the *Acadian Reporter* bitterly called the Maine city, "Canada's winter port."

PRIME MINISTER BORDEN ON SITE, OCTOBER 18, 1916. HE IS IN THE WHITE UNBANDED FEDORA, SPORTING A HEAVY MOUSTACHE.

Until 1913, Halifax's major wharves were in the North End. These were the big Richmond Seawall, the very important Naval Dockyard, and the great Deepwater Pier (1880) with its grain elevator at Cornwallis Street. But the election of Robert L. Borden as prime minister in 1911 was the beginning of the Ocean Terminals, the great South End development that promised to make Halifax "the New York of Canada." The city was elated. Confederation had been a disappointment and too much had been lost through de-industrialization. Nevertheless, some attempts to create industry had succeeded. The sugar refineries were surviving, and the 1889 graving dock was a success. But overall, too much had been lost, and protests were mounting.

Now, however, Borden was amenable to spending fifty-one million dollars on a brand-new port. First, a site had to be chosen. Deepwater in the North End was quickly ruled out; there was not much land left there and it would be very expensive to expropriate. Other sites were considered, including the Bedford Basin. Unfortunately, it was subject to ice and remote from the downtown. Dartmouth's waterfront was also possible, but without a bridge, how would the products get across the harbour? The ultimate reason for choosing the harbour in the South End was that the city's Armside was not well developed, and so could be bought or expropriated relatively cheaply. This area consisted mostly of a few old estates, imitative of the English country life, and the harbour slope was gentle between George's Island and Point Pleasant Park.

RAILWAY STEAM SHOVEL, C.1915

Work started with the turning of the first sod, July 31, 1913. The plan was to blast an eight-kilometre cut from Fairview in the city's far north end to Freshwater at its southern end and construct the Ocean Terminals, with its new seawall, big piers, and railway station costing one million dollars. The dynamited rubble was spread out at both ends. At Fairview, this helped create a large rail yard thirty-two tracks wide; at Freshwater, it filled the harbour's inset and moved the shore out half a kilometre, gave fill material for the piers, and created another large rail yard. The centrepiece was the two-thousand-foot seawall that could accommodate several of the largest ships simultaneously. Initially, although the track in the railroad cut would be double-tracked, there was provision for quadruple tracking. Since the cut interrupted a number of streets below Quinpool, temporary steel trestle bridges were thrown across. These were to be replaced by graceful concrete arches, the longest and last would be the double arch at Young Avenue.

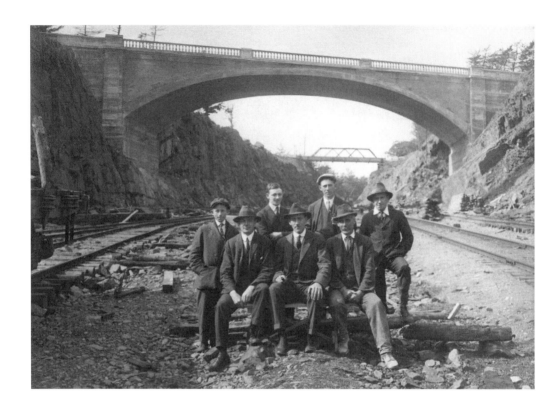

Blasting the fractured slate to make the cut presented problems. On July 15, 1914, the *Herald* reported that fifty thousand tons of rock had been moved with just nine tons of dynamite. But the Yacht Squadron, then closer to Freshwater than the breakwater, was bombarded with debris. Another bombardment on December 20, 1916, led to an injunction by residents of the Coburg Road and South Street area forbidding any flying debris, even if there was no damage. Also, while it was widely reported that no workers were killed during the blasting, apparently other deaths did not count. For example, on July 10, 1915, David Ursulan died after being hit by a falling timber. Then, on November 15, Roy Fleet suffered a horrible death when he was buried under eight feet of sand. He kept his hand over his face but was not rescued in time.

F.82. JULY.17.16.

Despite these deaths, the work continued. The seawall was built of hollow blocks, rubble filled, and faced with granite brought in from the Purcell's Cove quarry. The water depth was forty-five feet versus forty feet in New York and thirty-five in Boston. Borden laid the first sixty-two-ton block in October 1915. Piers A and B to the south were to be 1,500 feet, and to the south, near Greenbank, there would be a 1,500-foot-long breakwater. The new Intercolonial Railway station was to be near South Street. Plans called for a white marble campanile, or bell tower, like Saint Mark's Church in Venice. The overall plans were glorious. The results were somewhat less.

RAIL YARD CONSTRUCTION, c.1915

December 15, 1916, brought a sudden winter storm that tested the incomplete terminal. The breakwater handled it, but the first pier was not finished, lacking mooring posts and enough fenders to put between ships. The scows, dredges, and two larger ships were jammed into the quay using whatever fenders could be found. A sudden surge did it all—the ships banged and a scow went under. Despite this minor setback, progress was good, with the first stage finished by the summer of 1917, including at least one track to the proposed site of the station. This was fortunate for in December came the Halifax Explosion, and relief trains were able to come through the cut to the end of the track. A year-and-a-half later, the arrival of the first official train on December 23, 1918, was an event that drew crowds. The waving masses crowded the bridges, and officials met the train at the temporary station.

The Ocean Terminals, c.1925. Note an incomplete pier A and only the base of Pier B.

By 1920 much of the construction had been completed. Still, there were only temporary sheds on the piers, a temporary train station, a planned grain elevator, a proposed cold-storage plant and a still-to-be-built third pier at Greenbank. Then, in the summer of 1920, the post-war economy collapsed. Borden, exhausted by the war and the growing economic problems, resigned. His successor, Arthur Meighan, hapless and arrogant, suspended almost all new construction. The next year the Tories were defeated by William Lyon MacKenzie King. Initially, he did nothing either. Already, telephones had been removed from lighthouses "as an economy measure" and the navy disbanded. King, however, accepted Admiral Walter Hose's impassioned proposals and reversed the proposals, spending a modest amount on new ships for the navy. But still there was little funding for the Ocean Terminals.

Halifax's Ocean Terminals had been deserted. Gaunt red frames stood rusting against the empty blue sky. The only active places were the train station, which every fall sent thousands of young to the west on harvest excursions, and the incomplete piers, which had helped handle the overflow of thousands of returning soldiers in 1919–20. Nothing the locals could do seemed able to move Ottawa to complete the terminals.

**PRIME MINISTER
WILLIAM LYON
MACKENZIE KING,
C.1925**

Suddenly, in the fall of 1924, MacKenzie King announced new spending. The grain elevator would be built. The next year it was finished for $575,000, creating space for one million bushels. But, at least at first, no grain appeared. High freight rates allowed Saint John and especially Portland, Maine, to siphon too much. This happened despite Halifax being a day closer to both Europe and Latin America. The port, with its wonderful new elevator, was as busy "as a painted ship against a painted sky."

Dissatisfaction with the terminals helped lead to the Maritime Rights movement, a protest against economic policies that were felt to be unfair to the Maritime provinces. The federal response was the establishment of the Duncan Commission, which released a report in September 1926. It recommended a twenty percent cut in freight rates and further development of the ports of Saint John and Halifax. On the first of January 1928, the Halifax Harbour Commission was established. Suddenly, grain began to arrive. In fact, so much arrived that the elevator capacity was doubled by 1929. The recession that had started in the Maritimes in 1920 had lifted and the Roaring Twenties had arrived at last. Now many projects were being realized, including the Lord Nelson Hotel and Eaton's Department store.

THE COLD-STORAGE PLANT FROM THE TOWER ROAD BRIDGE, N.D.

The Ocean Terminals continued to develop. Halifax's big cold-storage plant appeared in 1928 at a cost of 2.5 million dollars. The Ocean Terminals sheds and railway station were finally finished. The seawall seemed a wonder in efficiency. Immigrants were received directly into the sheds from the ships, then sent by covered walkway to an adjacent immigration building for processing. Next they walked to the train station via a sheltered walkway. The immigration building even had a hospital where doctors and nurses had sleeping rooms and their own dining area. There were also detention rooms and, according to the Anglophone bias of that time, Britons were detained separately from non-Britons.

The one-and-a-half-storey railway shed was replaced with a concrete building, though without the gleaming campanile. Complementing it were the Nova Scotian Hotel and Cornwallis Park, created by tearing down the southern edge of Irishtown. Then, in 1929, Ottawa announced the four-million-dollar Pier B near Greenbank Cove. Shipping had increased dramatically. On February 11, 1929, for example, the *Mail* reported thirteen steamers in port. All the Ocean Terminals' docks were filled, as were three at Deepwater. The stevedores were fully employed.

The construction of Pier B was entertainment for many; the drills roared amid clouds of smoke and powerful dredges lifted the blasted and dripping residue. The dynamiters again got in trouble, this time for damaging the Berkeley Hotel on Inglis Street. An injunction put a halt to their fun. In the depressed summer of 1930, the sight of work gave hope. Unfortunately, there would be little in the next decade as the Depression told hold. World War Two brought life back to the waterfront, and the Ocean Terminals proved their worth, sending hundreds of thousands of troops overseas. Pier 21, the immigration shed, underutilized for its first twenty years, was very busy in the post-war period, receiving one million immigrants from war-torn Europe.

Stevedores were the elite of the unskilled and semi-skilled workers. In theory, they held the province in their thrall, for a well-timed strike could paralyze it. Yet, they rarely struck, unlike the dock workers of Saint John and Montreal. There were still difficulties between employer and worker. The *Acadian Recorder* of May 3, 1892, reported one as a "Laborers Difficulty." The men working for the West Indian Traders had to start at 6:00 a.m. But those working for the Government of Canada, the Intercolonial Railway, and the Imperial Government started at 7:00 a.m. The private employers agreed to the change in starting time, but resisted cutting the workday to nine hours from ten.

The stevedores' work was backbreaking and required a minimum of skill. The more skilled knew how to operate machinery and how to pack cargo so it did not shift and threaten the ship, but most only used brute force. They had few devices to ease their burden. Huge wheelbarrows weighing 150 to 200 pounds enabled the men to manipulate 600 pounds up sagging gangplanks.

Before the building of the Ocean Terminals, most of the work centered around the Deepwater port and its grain elevator at Cornwallis Street. As a result, stevedores tended to live on the waterfront, with Irishtown being fairly close. Later, they chose other cheap areas such as Richmond in the North End and Kline Heights in the hills overlooking the West End. Many, if not most, of the white stevedores were Irish Catholics, as was their leadership, men with names such as Joy, Sullivan, and Coolen. There was strict racial segregation between the blacks, who loaded coal, and the whites, who loaded freight. Stevedores were often seen at church on Sunday, and if they were not, the company paid their fine for working on the Sabbath. Dockers may not have been a good fit at an upper-middle-class dinner, but they were often good family men who struggled to support their wives and children with any work they could get. In summer, for example, they might go to Quebec City, or after 1931 to Churchill, Manitoba, where wages were very good. In fact, they might clear over four hundred dollars, enough to be able to take time off before returning to the Halifax waterfront. Their wives took in washing, kept chickens, or worked in the homes of the better off. The need for family labour was brought about by low wages, part-time work, lack of workers' compensation, no old age pensions, no employment insurance, and no hospital or medical insurance. It also meant the children of stevedores were often sent to work rather than to school. This lack of education trapped them in poverty and substandard housing. It also often forced the elderly to depend on their grown children.

Too often a stevedore might have less work due to the rare strike, or more frequently, injury. In the latter case, they initially had to rely on private welfare, such as the Saint Vincent de Paul Association. Later, Workers' Compensation would help in the event of injury, but payments were small and costs high. Wages varied according to circumstances. They were fifteen cents an hour and no holiday bonus in 1866, dropped to twelve-and-a-half cents in 1872, but rose to twenty-five cents an hour and double-time on Sundays by 1884. This was due to the Halifax Longshoremen's Association strike. These early unions were not stable, being formed and disbanded strike by strike. Therefore, it was 1907 before Local 269 of the International Longshoremen's Union was certified.

**DEEPWATER
PIER 2, C.1930**

Although the Halifax stevedores rarely went on strike, when they did they were clever. While labour disputes led to strikes as early as 1854—before they were legal—the strike of 1902 was an object lesson. Due to the erosion of wages since 1884, the men at Deepwater finally decided it was time to go out. Using a mix of union intimidation and Christian pacifism, they eventually forced concessions from the employer. The trouble began in late March. The still unrecognized longshoremen's union demanded higher wages, especially on Sundays, and four holidays with double pay. On March 14, a meeting held at Saint Patrick's Hall on Brunswick Street gained general labour support.

One of the big employers, Furness Withy, convinced itself that any increase would be ruinous. They claimed that traffic had not increased for years, then locked out their own stevedores on April's Fools Day and brought in strikebreakers. The union met the interlopers at the dock entrances and convinced many to join the strike or go home. Seventy joined on the first day. The strike was spreading and the whole harbour was threatened. The employers tried to use black workers to break the strike. It didn't work. Strikebreakers were called in from Eastern Passage. After sending their wives to shop downtown, they dropped down to the docks for a bit of extra money. The longshoremen managed to discourage, if not intimidate, them. Desperate, the employers brought in Bermudians and Italians from Sydney, trying to circumvent ethnic ties. Wrong again. The Longshoremen's Union suddenly ballooned from seven hundred to one thousand members. Even if the strikebreakers did not join the union, the Halifax boys had a strong incentive to convince them to go home after showing them how the companies had lied in saying the men were needed for a labour shortage. The union even provided the strikebreakers with train tickets and cheered them as they departed at the old North Street Station.

Meanwhile, the other unions met, praising the stevedores for their peaceful tactics. Deputy labour minister William Lyon MacKenzie King was telegraphed to come from Ottawa and "help the men in trouble." King had a spectacular career as a moderator between desperate trade unions and determined, angry employers. He agreed to intervene. By now almost the whole waterfront was on strike. The fish handlers, coalers, and coopers all walked. Suddenly, on April 9 the small operators at Deepwater and the Richmond Seawall relented, offering twenty-five cents during the day if the men returned immediately. These men did.

MacKenzie King arrived that same day. Forty-eight hours later, he had an agreement, becoming the union's hero. Wages were twenty cents in the day and twenty-five at night, double on Sunday and on the four holidays. The union was still below the 1884 day rate, but had equalled the night pay and gained the paid holidays and a non-retaliation clause. There was also an agreement that thirty days' notice would be given by either side before a strike or lockout. King not only won over the union, but also the employers. There would be another strike in 1907, and a near-strike in 1929, then virtually no trouble on the waterfront until the 1970s.

In December 1929, the nearly two thousand longshoremen gave thirty days' notice of not renewing their contract. They wanted new concessions including a nine-hour maximum shift, the same-sized gangs, lighter loads in the big wheelbarrows, ten cents extra for night work, and twenty-five cents more at cold storage, which they claimed was unhealthy, especially in summer. An impasse occurred, and the Federal Fair Wage Commissioner, Thomas V. Martin, was brought in. Simultaneously, the union suffered a major loss when president Michael D. Coolen died. He was buried at the Saint Patrick's Church on December 18, 1929. The Longshoremen attend en masse. The next day Martin got a settlement, and the union received a number of concessions.

THE CRUISE SHIP
***OLYMPIC* AT THE**
SEA WALL, N.D.

The Ocean Terminals had been the hope of both labour and capital. Initially, it never lived up to its billing, mainly because construction was so delayed. Eventually work was resumed and by 1934 the project was mostly finished. During the Great Depression, stevedore wages fell to sixty-three cents per hour. Wages would not recover until World War Two. Still, there were no strikes, therefore most South Enders were unaware of the docks except when large cruise ships such as the *Olympic* (pictured above) or battleships like the USS *Missouri* visited in the 1950s.

JOHN T. JOY,
c.1930

JOHN T. JOY
(Hon. President)

John T. Joy bridged the transition from Deepwater to the Ocean Terminals, becoming local union president in 1908. He finished his career with the Workers' Compensation Board, which he spearheaded. A member of Saint Mary's Cathedral Parish, Joy was deeply influenced by Catholic social doctrine, especially Pope Leo XIII's *Rerum Novarum,* "on the Condition of Labour." This encyclical, released in 1891, took a rather conservative approach to social justice. Rejecting class war, Leo also defended private property and the family as the bases of society. That said, he claimed that the state might have to intervene to protect the worker, who had a right to a living wage and the right to organize. This was news to many capitalists.

Joy's major contribution was in organizing the Workers' Compensation Board, so necessary in conception, so imperfect in application. For example, a 1911 act effectively forced workers to accept the opinion of the board's own doctors when most workers could not afford a second opinion. On top of this, the benefits were not very generous, although they slowly increased. Wages and conditions also improved during Joy's tenure, despite there having been no strikes. Workers could leave the pier after twenty hours without prejudice, and receive double time for work on munitions ships, for example. Today, Joy's name lives on with a Saint Mary's University scholarship administered by the Archdiocese of Halifax.

STEELS POND AND GREENBANK COVE, c.1888

Many South Enders remember Greenbank as a poor, run-down shantytown. But at one time, Greenbank was a desirable area. There was swimming in the cove and changing rooms nearby. As well, there were beautiful walks and inviting benches, and nearby Steel's Pond was a favourite skating area. Even the fashionable extreme south end of Pleasant Street, linking the city with Point Pleasant Park, ran through the area.

THE BAULD HOMES AND YACHT SQUADRON, OLD GREENBANK, c.1900

On Pleasant Street were some fine houses, including the two big Bauld homes on the west side. Between Greenbank and Freshwater was the Royal Nova Scotia Yacht Squadron at the Trider property. Also branching off Pleasant were a number of unfashionable streets, most of which have by now either disappeared or been renamed. Included were Clarence, Owen, Plover and View. Most of these would be buried under the 5-10 m of dynamited shale constituting the South End Rail yard. In the photo above, the Yacht Squadron is in its original South End location on the shore to the right. Beside is the home of Mrs. J. C. MacIntosh.

Greenbank became a tarpaper village by about 1915 when the Intercolonial Railway built a typical railway shantytown without any running
water. When the railway was finished, dockers remained and took over
the shacks. There were about twenty-eight houses near the intersection
of Clarence and Brussels Streets. The shacks at that corner conformed to
the streets and had street numbers, but away from it, they were scattered
higgledy-piggledy. Most had tar and gravel roofs. The largest home, with
a veranda around it, was that of Harold Scallion, who worked for the
CNR. There was also a store near the edge of the cut run by the March-
ands. Otherwise, there was nothing but shacks. Some, just to the south
in Miller's Field, had been built as temporary shelter for victims of the
Halifax Explosion. They were not taken down until Greenbank was. In
the rail yard, where the railways split between those going to the station,
and those going to Pier B, was an island with four more buildings and a
steel power tower. This was, to use Bill Mont's term, "Dogpatch." The
residents could only safely reach the city by walking toward Terminal
Road in the ever-widening gap between the rails.

GREENBANK FROM STEEL'S POND, 1934. DR. WILFRED CREIGHTON IS USING THE FIREHOSE.

The buildings in Greenbank should have only lasted a few years but some lingered until 1956. Rent was paid to the slumlord, Mrs. Susan Mack, widow of the well-known doctor, Joshua N. Mack. They were the first family on Ogilvie Street. She charged five dollars per month for a two-room cottage without *any* city services. The residents of Greenbank worked at a variety of jobs, many of them on the nearby docks. But there were other jobs. There were two bakeries on Tower Road— Bens Bakery had a substantial business in the big wood apartment building at Fay's Lane while Stanhopes had a small bakery at the rear of number 36. Among the Greenbankers who probably worked there were the bakers Albert and Mike Bellfountain. Alfred Smith was a soldier with the Royal Canadian Regiment. Daniel Hull was a sailor, and Willis Rhynhart a gardener at one of the big homes or estates. Charles O'Neil painted with the CNR, Earl Malloy was a machinist at Purdy Brothers Car Shop on Morris Street, and Fred Dowling was a firefighter.

Unlike Africville, to which it was often compared, Greenbank had no community school nor community church. Therefore, the major focus seemed to be the little store. There were two schools in the general area, but they were split on religious lines—Tower Road was for the non-Catholics and College Street for the others. This lack of common institutions reduced Greenbank's ability to be as strong a community as Africville was, although Greenbank has had a number of reunions. On the other hand, there was a baseball field on Miller Street. In the twentieth century, the Greenbankers also played ball on the Tramways Field at Francklyn Park with the guys from Tower Road. The Greenbankers called themselves the "Aces," the Tower Road boys were no-names. Occasionally, girls also played.

In 1956 after only two generations, Greenbank disappeared. Some residents moved to Spryfield using wood from the old shacks to build anew. Today, Greenbank is replaced by a large apartment building, Ogilvie Towers, featuring a view of the park to the south, of the docks and rail yards to the northeast.

Chapter 6

The New South End

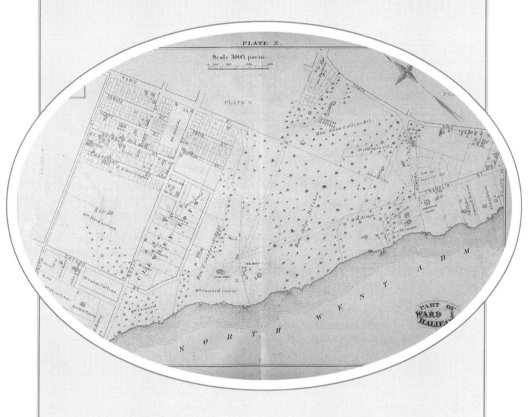

HOPKINS ATLAS, SHOWING THE ESTATES OF THE NEW SOUTH END, C.1878

The New South End consists of those homes and institutions in the southwest corner of the peninsula—west of Tower Road and below South Street. Its major development dates from just before World War One. This area includes Saint Mary's University and the related area of upper-middle-class homes in Francklyn Park and is physically separated from the Old South End by Collins Field. The New South End replaced the Old South End as the home of the upper-middle class. Many of the city's most impressive estates were located in the New South End, especially in the area near the Arm, at one time considered the city's prime summer vacation spot.

AERIAL MAP OF THE NEW SOUTH END, SHOWING POINT PLEASANT PARK, 1931

In the aerial map above, the Gorsebrook Golf Course is the large field in the northwest quadrant. Immediately to the south is the future Saint Mary's University campus, also part of the golf course. The area between SMU and the railway is Marlborough Woods, now covered with houses. The prominent road to the centre-left of the Gorsebrook field is Oakland.

Strangely, the New South End grew from the west. Originally it consisted of a series of English country estates dating back to the late eighteenth century, where the residents preferred to live in splendid isolation on the western edge of the peninsula. Then, coincident with the rebuilding of Halifax in the 1850s and 1860s, a building boom of the old estates on the Arm occurred. A major example of rebuilding was Oaklands, built anew at the time of the American Civil War by William Cunard, son of the founder of the famous steamship line. He maintained his British outlook, with his family business in England. Eventually, Cunard would move there to take care of it.

It was only the twentieth century that brought the extensive development of New South End. The first attempt was the North West Arm Land Company's failed proposal for Marlborough Woods in the 1890s. It was to populate the wooded area west of Robie and below Oakland. A bit later there came the more successful Gorsebrook Golf Course, which dated from 1896 as the Halifax Golf Club. Then, in the early 1920s, there was the Oakland subdivision, a potential rival to Young Avenue. Also in the 1920s, Inglis Street west of Robie started to develop, but it was only following the Second World War that Marlborough Woods completely disappeared under hundreds of upper-middle-class homes.

Enos Collins bought the Gorsebrook property in 1821 and became its most well-known owner. The house was on Tower Road, while the estate extended from the Bower in the south to the edge of the South Common on South Street and from modern Robie Street in the west to Tower Road in the east. The house had three floors, four bedrooms on the upper level, dining and living areas on the main floor and food storage and pantries in the cellar. To the west, there was a long extension with separate quarters for servants. The barn was further west toward Robie Street, but the farm gate was near the modern Gorsebrook Avenue on Tower Road. The chief outcome of the house's destruction was the founding of the Heritage Trust of Nova Scotia.

Collins almost left Nova Scotia in the early 1820s because of the post-war depression. An appointment to the Council of Twelve (the appointed upper house of the legislature) and the arranged marriage to Margaret Haliburton, daughter of Sir Brenton Haliburton, kept him in the province, where he became part of the local oligarchy that ruled the colony to its own advantage.

In his old age, Collins would often be seen sitting on his veranda looking at his hill, his gout-swollen legs wrapped in bandages. He would see the poor homes on Lundy's Lane and his fields, never dreaming that his descendant, Carteret Fitzgerald Collins, would rent it to a golf course. Near the end of his life, Collins would also see the massive bulk of the Poor House rise on South Street. His estate was split in 1894 when the city drove Inglis Street across it chiefly to serve the interests of the North West Arm Land Company, which was trying to develop Marlborough Woods. Collins's administrator, Robie Uniacke, weakly protested but would not seek legal action. He also pointed out that North West Arm's plan to run the electric tram to the Arm was unrealistic as there were virtually no homes between Tower Road and the water. The city went ahead with the plan, but made the company bear the costs.

Collins Hill (later Gorsebrook Hill) has been a scene of winter sports for almost a century and a half. But there was danger there. On February 18, 1878, the *Morning Chronicle* reported that a number of people were coasting on a moonlit Friday night when a toboggan crashed into a military officer, dislocating his leg. A year later, on February 7, 1879, a gunsmith's apprentice was knocked cold by a careening sled. At least the City and Provincial Hospital was only half a block northeast.

GATHERING AT THE BELMONT GOLF HOUSE, 1904   Collins's estate stayed in his family for the next generations. In 1900, the northern half was rented to the Gorsebrook Golf Club. Initially, there were only nine holes. The clubhouse was the old Belmont Gate House, the double grey bungalow on Robie Street between Oakland Road and the Belmont Trail, now Belmont Road. Until it was converted into a residence, the floors still showed spike marks. In the photo of the course below, the large building in the background is the Poor House. The birches still exist today.

On the Golf Course, Halifax, N.S.

THE GORSEBROOK GOLF COURSE LOOKING NORTH, N.D.

In the mid-1920s, the club established a temporary clubhouse at the future site of Saint Francis School with a deck facing Collins Hill. This was just a stopgap, for in 1928 the Collins estate rented out the lower half and the course expanded to a short eighteen holes. "Sam" Foley, the club's professional, designed the course. No trees were to be cut, therefore, number seventeen was only thirty feet wide, hemmed in by towering trees, and only 125 yards long. Number sixteen at 160 yards long had a fifteen-foot drop and number eighteen had a stone wall on the left. On the other hand, the players received a fine clubhouse, Collins's old house. The members revelled in its appointments, the fireplaces, the fine old-fashioned dining room in green with green tables, the windows both high and deep. They thought it had an English feel and appreciated the extra space. Still, an addition was made for the men's changing room; the women received the modified basement. Teas remained social events that even required a professional caterer.

When Ashburn announced in 1922 that it would build a regular eighteen-hole course and Brightwood went to eighteen holes in 1924, there was talk of closing the short Gorsebrook. Instead it was reconstituted as a community golf course with low rates. The upper-middle class made sure they dominated.

Gerald and Frank Mielke were working-class boys from the poor area of Wellington Street who worked at the shipyards. The Mielkes learned their game at Gorsebrook, but mostly played at Brightwood. The two went on to win the Maritime Amateur Championship, reaching their limit at the Canadian Championships where they did well but failed to win, partly because they could not afford to practice full-time.

The only player from Gorsebrook who could match them was the young pro, "Sam" Foley.

He also ran a winter course in a downtown Halifax building that attracted players not only from Gorsebrook, but also from Ashburn and Brightwood. Foley was the first to beat par when Gorsebrook expanded to eighteen holes, hitting an extremely low fifty-nine on July 8, 1930. Of course, it helped that he had designed the course. Among the women there were also several outstanding players. While the well-known Edith Bauld, probably from Pleasant Street, played Ashburn, she had her Gorsebrook equivalent, the younger, but more matronly, Mrs. D. Leo Dolen, originally from Glace Bay. Dolen became women's champion at Gorsebrook in 1928 and gave Bauld a run for her money. She only played one year at Gorsebrook then also switched to Ashburn.

The Gorsebrook Golf Course trundled along until World War Two when it became obvious that it could not last. Carteret Fitzgerald Collins died in Tunbridge Wells, England, in 1941 and the sell-off began. Saint Mary's College took legal possession of the half below Inglis in 1943. The college continued to lease it to the club until it was almost ready to start construction on their new campus in 1949. By the end of the war, RCAF Gorsebrook had encroached on the northeast corner, reducing the course to a desperate and odd thirteen holes. The city had bought the remainder of the northern half of the Collins estate and soon would divide it into baseball diamonds before building Gorsebrook School in 1949. The club was almost dead, but had its last nine-hole course at Saint Mary's University for the 1948 season. The Gorsebrook Golf Club closed after the season and the field north of Inglis that had been part of the course became the possession of the people, effectively replacing, in part, the lost South Common.

THE ROAD FROM BAZALGETTE'S HOME TO FRESHWATER BRIDGE, C.1840

Almost completely forgotten is the Bazalgette Estate that bordered on Collins's land (later called Belvedere). Colonel John Bazalgette was born in 1784 in London, the descendant of a noble French family that had settled in England during the eighteenth century. He came to Nova Scotia in 1811, where he was twice acting governor of Nova Scotia, first in 1846 then again from 1851–52, when he dissolved the legislature to allow the Liberals to form the government and implement Joe Howe's railway bill. His house was built in about 1811 by John Trider from the lumber of the old 1759 Government House. This led to the house being termed "Bazalgette's parliament." Belvedere was at the southwest corner of Tower Road and Inglis Street.

Bazalgette bought it in about 1817 and made additions for his very large family. Belvedere had a splendid view of the harbour and citadel. There was a coach house and stables, a garden and a hot house. The house itself had a fine drawing room, library, butler's pantry, large dining room, basement kitchen, and southern veranda. There were six bedrooms on the second floor and four in the attic. His estate was only twenty-one acres consisting, in addition to the house site, of the north side of what would become Inglis, west to Wellington Street, and up Wellington to South Street. Bazalgette died in London on March 21, 1868. Some of his children remained and rose to prominent positions in the city. Today, however, the name is extinct in the area.

Maplewood, c.1900

Nova Scotia senator and lieutenant-governor David MacKeen's big house, Maplewood, was built in 1870. The house had fourteen rooms, a small conservatory, and later, a fine ballroom.

It was rented for most of its existence. At one time, it was hoped the Governor General would make it a summer residence. In 1896 Mac-Keen bought the place for thirteen thousand dollars, and at his wife's request rebuilt the house in grand style. The house remained in the family until early 1974 when it suspiciously burned just after it was sold. Maplewood was the last of the great Armside estates to disappear from the new South End.

On August 24, 1891, "Lady Jane" wrote a newspaper story about a man with a camera not far from MacKeen's Maplewood. She claimed he followed the laughing down to the Arm and saw what appeared to be mermaids cavorting in the water and sitting on the rocks in dripping, clinging garments. The photographer developed the photos and discovered "society in déshabille!" Lady Jane suggested money was to be made and that she knew the photographer, but, of course, was sworn to secrecy.

The original Belmont House was built by Captain Henry G. Duncan about 1790. He named it after his ancestral home in Scotland. In 1811 John Howe, Jr., postmaster and half-brother to politician Joe, bought the fire-damaged house for one thousand pounds. Having repaired it, this public-spirited owner allowed community groups to use the property. For example, in August 1837 Howe had the Union Fire Company where he was captain, as his guests for their picnic.

JUDGE JOHN RITCHIE, C.1880

DR. ELIZA RITCHIE, N.D.

After Howe's death in 1842, Belmont ended up in the hands of Scott Tremaine, who tried to develop the property for housing. Having failed, he died and it passed to Judge John Ritchie for a steep three thousand pounds. The original house was replaced by a large Gothic house built by Henry Elliot and Henry F. Bush circa 1864. Its form was partially masked by a large enclosed porch. The entire Belmont Estate was about ninety-three acres, of which thirty-six were cultivated. The property had a fine growth of hard and softwood surrounded by a stone wall, which is still apparent today in the backyards on Beaufort. When Ritchie died in 1890, he left the estate to his widow and three sons.

In the 1890s, Armside estates were fashionable in summer. Lady Jane complained tongue-in-cheek in the *Acadian Recorder* of April 29, 1893, that Morris Street was "not nearly as fashionable as before," since everyone was leaving for the Arm. James Morrison was going to that "tiny box," Coburg Cottage; Mr. and Mrs. Walter Jones had left for the Bower; Captain and Mrs. Clarkson were renting Maplewood, which Lady Jane thought would make an ideal hotel; and finally, Colonel and Mrs. Leach had taken Oaklands.

Judge Ritchie was not the only prominent Haligonian connected to the Armside estates. In fact, his daughter, Eliza Ritchie, was considered one of the most important leaders of the women's movement in Halifax. She became Nova Scotia's first female professor when she began teaching Sanscrit at Dalhousie and was later the first woman on the university's board of governors. Ritchie was lived at Winwick, an offshoot of Belmont. The house later had two Royal visits when Premier Angus L. Macdonald was the resident. Ritchie died on September 4, 1933.

OAKLANDS
ESTATE, C.1890

William Taylor built the Oaklands Estate in 1786. At forty acres, it was less than half the size of Belmont, but had a much more impressive home on the Arm and a gatehouse on Robie. William Cunard, son of the founder of the Cunard Steamship Company, moved from Brunswick Street in 1864 and rebuilt Oaklands. In style, it was Italianate with a central tower and round-topped windows. Constructed of brick, the basement was granite with freestone trim. The interior was made of walnut, cherry, mahogany, and birch. Measuring ninety feet by forty-five feet, the house had three storeys above ground and was worth $150,000, or six times what Hobrecker's later castle on Young Avenue or W.H. Bauld's mansion on south Pleasant were worth.

After Cunard left for England and Oaklands passed through several other hands, it became a victim of the Ocean Terminals. The railway was planned to run right through the estate. At this point, developer F. B. McCurdy, smelling a deal, bought the home for a mere $1,250, then tried to move it for $15,000. The house was raised on two hundred jacks and rails were laid for the quarter-mile journey south into Marlborough Woods. But unfortunately, McCurdy was soon smelling not a deal, but smoke, for on December 29, 1914, the house burned under suspicious circumstances.

Oakland Road originally appeared as early as the 1860s as part of the aborted attempt to develop the Clewley Estate on South Street. As early as January 20, 1783, the estate of John Clewley was mentioned in the

Royal Gazette. By 1815 his executor was offering lots along what would become South Street. These lots extended down to Oaklands. They were said to be "extremely capable of cultivation, [and] were excellent for country houses." By mid-century a dozen lots had been taken, and in general, the area was starting to develop.

By 1865 Oakland Road ran down from South, then west toward what would become Oxford Street. There were a few houses on South, or Clewley Road, with circular drives, but nothing on the modern Cartaret or Oakland except Cunard's three apparent servants' homes on the south side of Oakland. It was not until 1913 that a connection with Robie was made, creating a straight road to the railway cut. In 1910 Oakland Road received running water and sewers, despite only having two houses. This caused some opposition, but without these services development would have been delayed. The street grew slowly through the next twenty years of war, post-war recession, the Great Depression, and rutted roads. It was not filled comfortably until about 1940.

Oakland Road never was a serious rival to Young Avenue. There is no evidence of Oakland enforcing legal restrictions on development like on Young Avenue or Connaught, where the developers had private bills passed in the legislature to create "properly protected properties." What happened on Oakland is what happens when there are no rules. On the south side between Robie and Bellevue Avenue are several small cottages. Even more bizarre was Graham Pace's service station at the corner of Waterloo that lasted from 1930 to 1939. Not many remember it, and no wonder. It was in a deep hollow, with the top of the station almost at street level and a house shielding it from Oakland Road.

Chapter 7

The West End Goes South

HOPKINS ATLAS, HALIFAX'S WEST END

The West End Pharmacy at Spring Garden and Robie, the West End Grocery on Jubilee, and the West End Baptist Church on Quinpool Road all indicate that, before World War Two, the area bounded by South Street, Robie Street, Quinpool Road and the Northwest Arm was known as the West End. Nevertheless, with the post-war development of the Westmount subdivision on the old Halifax airport site and the building of the Halifax Shopping Centre, Bayers Road Shopping Centre, and West End Mall, this new area became the new West End. Orphaned, the old West End became part of the South End. Therefore, although today some locals occasionally refer to the area as the West End, most of the time the term refers to post-war development in the northwest peninsula.

The old West End, like the New South End, is residential, but it predates the latter. The old West End was originally lower-middle class, closer to Schmidtville in its economic level. Further west on Oxford Street, the Edwardian upper-middle class built many fine and large homes. Around the time of World War Two, houses similar to those in the New South End filled the remaining area west of Oxford, where there were also a number of Armside estates. In between, the area even developed its own version of Young Avenue, Rosebank Park, whose centre is Connaught Avenue.

ALEXANDER CROKE, c.1810

The Studley Estate, bounded by South and Oxford streets, Coburg Road, and LeMarchant Street, was not on the Arm, but on the hill high above. Studley was built in 1802 by Judge Alexander Croke, the acerbic critic of colonial officials and churchmen. The eleven-room house was on a steep, rocky hill crowned by pines. The estate was self-sufficient, a place where Croke could retire after a day in court, or administering the colony. Once home, Croke could vent his spleen on the foibles of his contemporaries, including Bishop Charles Inglis, and the not-so-gentle Nova Scotia winter.

**STUDLEY HOUSE,
1930**

In 1816, Croke retired to England, and in 1831, the *Nova Scotian* reported the unintentional destruction of Studley. Soot in the chimney was being burned when defective mortar near the roof caused the building to catch fire. Studley, like the other Arm estates, was too far from the town centre to be saved. By the time the army arrived, the building, worth 1,500 pounds, was lost. Only the furniture was saved. Matthew Richardson later rebuilt the house, and even later Dr. Robert Murray gave it its best-known name, the Murray homestead. In 1913 Dalhousie received the forty-one-acre estate. The house was demolished in 1949 for the Arts and Administration Building, now the Henry Hicks Building. Studley was also the home of the former Halifax Golf Club, a very small nine-hole course that existed from 1896 to 1900. The "nineteenth hole" was on LeMarchant.

William Pryor, a West Indian merchant, at one time owned all the land along the Arm from Quinpool Road to South Street. Pryor Street, near Jubilee, is named after him. He bought the land from Major General John Campbell and built his house "Jubilee" in 1810. Its name commemorated George III's fifty years.

WILLIAM PRYOR,
c.1840

COBURG HOUSE,
c.1880

Pryor's land was divided into a number of estates: Thornvale, Blenheim, Bircham/Birchdale, Bloomingdale, Rosebank, Jubilee, and Armdale. There was also Hillside on Jubilee and Coburg House, which existed from 1816 and was later Sir Sanford Fleming's home. When Pryor died, much of his property was divided. One of his sons, Henry, a magistrate, retained a portion of the estate, where he built Hillside.

THORNVALE,
c.1880

Thornvale, much closer to South Street than Coburg, was the home of
T. E. Kenny, son of Sir Edward Kenny and first president of the Royal
Bank. In 1867 he replaced the 1828 cottage of William Pryor, Jr., with
a three-storey home whose lower walls were covered in ivy. Thornvale
Avenue is named after it.

BLENHEIM COTTAGE, C.1880

Blenheim Cottage was more than a cottage. It was built in 1871 by the young William Duffus for his bride. The "cottage" had nine bedrooms, twenty-two gabled windows, a very high, sloping, curved roof, two fantasy chimneys at either end, a curving veranda at the top, and a grand staircase. This extreme exaggeration of the Second Empire style was a wonder to some, but probably something else to others. Three years after he built it, Duffus sold the house to Sandford Fleming. Long-time owner Sir Sandford Fleming and his family are pictured here on the front lawn.

BLOOMINGDALE, c.1890. SHOWS EAST SIDE BEFORE EXPANSION BY WAEGWOLTIC CLUB.

Bloomingdale, the home of Lieutenant-Governor Alfred Giplin Jones, a son-in-law of William Stairs, was built in 1861. Jones's children were talented artists. Alice, a novelist, still has works in libraries, and Frances, an artist, still has displayed works. Bloomingdale Limited bought the house and established what was later called the Waegwoltic Club. They enlarged the building for a dining room to the north in a complementary style. The club opened in May 1908.

It was at Fairfield that the Victorian hero Captain William Stairs was raised. He accompanied Henry Stanley on the not-very-necessary rescue of Governor Emin Pasha of the Turkish Equatoria. The Arm crowd celebrated anyway, since the expedition was lost to the world for two years of tropical diseases, aggressive jungle animals, and hostile natives. In 1910 Fairfield was taken over by the Saint Mary's Total Abstinence and Benevolent Society, which established it as a social club. The house was demolished in 1930 and replaced by Villa Maria, the archbishop's palace, which was somehow built in the Great Depression. At least it provided much-needed work, even for its famous architect, Andrew Cobb. In 1919 the part of Fairfield immediately north of Villa Maria became Saint Mary's Boat Club. Wisely, the city maintained the shoreline below Villa Maria, increasing public access to the Arm. This reduced the potential shoreline of the Waeg by almost fifty percent.

The Jubilee Estate was built by William Pryor and later became most closely associated with Isabella Binney Cogswell. A very retiring person who found meaning in philanthropy, Cogswell founded the Halifax Industrial School for troubled boys and helped establish the Old Lady's Home on Gottingen Street for widows of Anglican clergy, a building which still stands today as Victoria Hall, a large red wooden building above the street. Cogswell died on December 7, 1874, at age fifty-five. Jubilee was the only estate other than Oaklands to be destroyed by the railway cut.

Rosebank, built in 1818 and immediately up Jubilee Road from Cogswell's Jubilee Estate, was once the 1786 country home of the local military commander, Major John Campbell. The estate received its name from the Bingen Rose, the emblem of his regiment in the Seven Years' War. Rosebank featured a sandstone wall and the gateposts had the rose in stone, the estate's landmarks for a century. In 1912 thirty acres of the estate's forty became Rosebank Park, with its centrepiece Connaught Avenue. The southwest corner was lost to the railway cut.

The Almons were the best known and most controversial of Rosebank's owners. Doctor William Johnston Almon was a supporter of the Confederacy. In 1864, in the middle of the American Civil War, his son, William Bruce, volunteered as a doctor for the South and was appointed as assistant surgeon at the Lady's Hospital at Columbia, South Carolina. As the Yankees advanced, Almon escaped to Florida where he was captured. After his release, he returned to Nova Scotia, where he died two years later of consumption on February 1, 1867, at only twenty-six years old.

DR. WILLIAM ALMON, C.1880

ARMDALE HOUSE, c.1885

The last estate on the south side of Quinpool Road was Armdale, built by Henry Peters who had bought the land from Henry Pryor in about 1864. The Neo-Classical building had three storeys with lots of "gingerbread" under the eaves. One of its most famous owners was Dr. Charles Tupper, who later went off to Ottawa where he spent a very short ten weeks as prime minister in 1896. The Sir Charles Tupper Medical Building at Dalhousie University commemorates his work as a physician.

CALDWELL HOUSE, c.1930

Just north of Jubilee Road was William Caldwell's home. The house was designed by Henry G. Hill in the 1840s in the Greek Revival style. It had a temple form, but with a hipped roof—a Maritime touch. In 1851 Caldwell was elected mayor, and was known for having fired a cannon at Camp Hill for over one-and-a-half hours on Dominion Day 1867 to celebrate Confederation.

FIELDS WEST OF OXFORD, c.1880

Much of Oxford Street was undeveloped in 1878. The upper reaches of Oxford were still mostly fields, with a few cottages, until the street became developed at the end of the nineteenth century. At that time many upper-middle-class homes appeared, especially on the later-developing west side. Closer to Quinpool Road, the housing was more pedestrian.

OAKVILLE, N.D.   Just below Coburg Road were the twin houses of John T. Wylde, "Arm-brae," and Levi Hart, "Oakville." Oakville still stands in its Italianate glory, and is home of the president of Dalhousie University.

NORTH WEST ARM CLUB, C.1906

Closely related to the fine estates in the Old West End were the Arm clubs, slow to develop during the nineteenth century. In the summer of 1867 the *Acadian Recorder* complained about Sunday recreation, using the drowning of a young man as its vehicle for calling for police to enforce the Blue Laws, which forbade such activity on the Sabbath. More legitimate were the semi-official Banker's Regattas, which were held from the 1870s to the early 1900s, and skating on the sometimes "capital ice." Still, the Arm was apparently not well known by the public until the twentieth century. The Arm clubs were the Northwest, Saint Mary's, the Waegwoltic, and the Jubilee at Hillside Estate.

The first club on the Arm was the 1899 North West Arm Rowing Club at the foot of South Street, opposite Thornvale. There were 198 berths, and a big, two-storey boathouse with the Union Jack, Royal Navy, and club flags stiffening in the breeze. Boats could also be hired. In 1906 the popular club added forty-eight more berths for boats and opened a lunchroom in the clubhouse area. The North West Arm Club was demolished in 1978.

SAINT MARY'S BOAT CLUB, C.1925

Near the end of Jubilee Road appeared the Saint Mary's Boat Club. It occupied the northern part of the Fairfield Estate. In an age where it was felt necessary to have "separate but equal" facilities based on religion, there was not only a separate Catholic school but also separate Catholic organizations within the sports world. One of these was the Saint Mary's Aquatic Club, commonly called Saint Mary's Boat Club. Founded in 1900, the club was a refugee, moving from site to site before finally finding its own land in 1919.

Saint Mary's continued until the late twentieth century. The membership was mostly from the immediate area, but a number of North Enders also belonged. By World War Two, however, with so many men away, club memberships declined as they did at the other clubs. The club came back after the war, holding well-attended teen dances in the 1950s and early 1960s. But it lost its way later, becoming a drop-in centre for youth, then in 1972, a youth hostel. The only thing that seemed to symbolize the old club was the lawn bowling. After a couple of decades of neglect, the clubhouse was upgraded and the club's facilities hold the South End's summer recreation programs.

JOHN O'NEILL,
c.1905

From the beginning, the Saint Mary's Aquatic Club emphasized sports. Saint Mary's hero, and indeed the Arm's, was John O'Neill, the greatest rower since George Brown. On August 7, 1909, O'Neill won the North American singles championship in Detroit. Five days later, the Arm clubs held another great celebration. There were bonfires, and hundreds of boats had lights. Birchdale Hotel held a reception, and when O'Neill arrived at the club after the civic reception, he wore the Saint Mary's colours, green and black. It was a great day for the Arm.

Established in 1908, the Waegwoltic Boat Club, under the presidency of John W. Reagan, author of *Sketches and Traditions of the Northwest Arm*, became very popular. Today, it is the only private club left on the east side of the Arm. The Waegwoltic grounds were designed by Richard Power of the Public Gardens. Others joined and took shares in the Bloomfield Company, but single women could join as "privileged members," so didn't have to take shares. In 1912 there were 510 members but only 35 privileged. The manager earned seven hundred dollars while the groundskeeper received forty dollars per month. Occasionally, there were discipline problems—William Wickwire lost his membership for public drunkenness. The club boasted sailing, swimming, quoits, and tennis, among other sports. Unfortunately, the Arm was not noted for its warmth, therefore by the 1920s the Waeg had a swimming pool. A heated swimming pool still graces the club today, although quoits has disappeared.

In the aftermath of the Halifax Explosion, the Waeg was a temporary hospital, its size being a factor. The directors had to meet elsewhere, and on February 19, 1918, they asked for use of the property by March 1. The need was such that the hospital did not vacate the premises until early May. For many, the Waeg's biggest day was when it hosted the arrival of the Prince of Wales in August 1919. The clubhouse was closed to ordinary members for the event, which ran from Saturday evening until Monday evening.

This club of the well-to-do was not immune to the local economy. In the severe recession of the 1920s, membership fell twenty percent from a high of 915 in 1921 to 740 in 1926. After recovering during the period from 1927–1930, the membership plunged over forty percent during the Great Depression, falling from 800 in 1930 to only 462 in 1934. Complicating efforts to boost membership was the state of the Arm itself. By the mid-1930s, Arm pollution was impossible to ignore. In 1916 the Waeg had given a thirty-foot strip to the Northwest Arm Sewer to help move the outfall from Coburg Road to Chain Rock, the depths near the mouth of the Arm. Three years later the sewer had not been finished so the club contacted the city. Reassurances were received, but Halifax was rebuilding the devastated North End, and the post-war recession was just below the horizon. Halifax could not find the money to finish the sewer immediately. Although the sewage diversion was eventually finished, it was plain to most that the move was inadequate. A generation later, on November 15, 1956, with the Arm pollution again terrible, the directors passed a resolution that was sent to the mayor in the club's name and signed by the other clubs. Coliform bacteria counts had confirmed that which had been sensed. Despite the ruined Arm, the Waeg survived. By 1958 there were five tennis courts, two saltwater pools, quoit bed, a canteen, a hundred berths for small boats and 1,600 single members, not to mention many more families.

There have been persistent rumours that the early Waegwoltic discriminated against Jews. Certainly, by the time that Halifax's first Jewish mayor, Leonard Kitz (1955–57), was elected, discrimination seemed to be gone. Unfortunately, this was not so. According to *Barometer Magazine*, a late-1970s journal, the Waeg had in 1964 refused for membership a former RCAF man who was Jewish, but was willing to admit a German who had fought for the Luftwaffe. Long before, similar clubs such as the Oakfield Golf Club had specifically outlawed such outrageous behaviour. The Waeg was not always at the forefront of social progress.

Not far away, another South End development, Rosebank Park, also failed to take off quickly. The federal government had abandoned the Ocean Terminals when the post-war inflation collapsed in 1920, not resuming construction again until 1924. The Maritimes had entered a recession that was only broken in 1927–30 by a mini-boom. Then all was lost as the world plunged into the Great Depression. Rosebank Park, along with many other projects, stalled. It would be the 1940s before most of the lots were filled. Rosebank Park had begun as an equivalent to Young Avenue, but this never quite happened.

FIRST BAPTIST CHURCH, OXFORD STREET, C.1952

Originally, there was also a plan to extend Connaught Avenue from Jubilee Road to Robie Street in a great arc parallel to the Arm. With the blasting of the railway canyon, plans had to be fine-tuned. Then the recession of the 1920s and the Great Depression kept the idea theoretical until after World War Two. By then houses had been built on the east side of the proposed road. Those between Regina Terrace and Inglis had been set back fifty feet from the road in anticipation. Nevertheless, by 1950 the idea was dead, and the new First Baptist Church was built in the proposed path, just above South on Oxford.

Marching to Saint Andrew's United Church, c.1943

After a fire destroyed the old First Baptist Church, Baptists had worshipped at Saint Andrew's United Church Hall on Coburg until the simple but beautiful Gothic replacement was opened on Easter Sunday 1950. Other churches in the Old West End included Saint Stephen's chapel of ease, completed in 1887, and Saint Andrew's United, which replaced the old church on Tobin Street.

The first school in the West End was LeMarchant, built in 1887 for the rapidly developing area around Coburg Road. After the opening of St. Thomas Aquinas Church, the Catholics built a separate school on Watt Street across from LeMarchant, also called St. Thomas Aquinas, in 1927. The Sir Charles Tupper School, designed to take the overflow from Quinpool Road School, was one of the last schools built during the Depression, opening in 1930. Nineteen years later, to fill the gap between LeMarchant and Sir Charles Tupper, Cornwallis Junior High School was built at Preston and Cedar.

Chapter 8

The Military and the South End

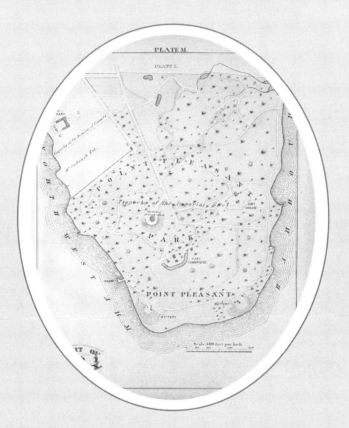

HOPKINS ATLAS: POINT PLEASANT PARK, 1878

Most Haligonians know of Stadacona and Windsor Park, the prominent North End navy and army military bases, and Shearwater, the air base across the harbour. Few think of the South End having much to do with the military. However, most of Halifax's Victorian forts were in Point Pleasant Park, and until recently, the former Navy League Building at Barrington and South Streets was the command centre for World War Two naval operations in the Northwest Atlantic. There were also the army and air force residence on College Street, the air force residence on Gorsebrook Field, and the Seaward Defence Base, with its sea mines, near Steel's Pond. In fact, until about 1950 the South End was a major military area. Also underappreciated was that the South End was affected by the 1917 Halifax Explosion—the damage did not suddenly stop at Citadel Hill. A number of buildings were severely damaged, including Morris Street School, where twenty-one died. The area's damaged but still mostly intact hospitals became major treatment centres for the devastated North End.

The naval dockyard was formally established in 1759 to aid in operations against Louisbourg and Quebec. The decade previous, Edward Cornwallis had written the Duke of Bedford suggesting the establishment of batteries at Sandwich (Point Pleasant) and on the opposite side of the Northwest Arm. One result was the 1762 battery, with a chain stretched across the Arm, the origin of the Northwest Arm Battery at Chain Rock. Later, as the French threat of war reappeared, the park's military presence became more prominent. In 1794, for example, Fort Ogilvie was built. It had six twenty-pound cannons, a guard house, and a furnace to heat the shot.

It was 1795 when Prince Edward, Duke of Kent, appeared. The best of a bad lot of sons of Charlotte Sophie and the sometimes-mad George III, Edward left Halifax better built than he found it. Exiled to the colonies for his indiscretions, Edward was determined to regain his father's favour. He rebuilt the military structure in Point Pleasant Park, updated the Citadel, and constructed a love nest for his mistress, Julie St. Laurent, at Prince's Lodge. Edward's only legitimate child became Queen Victoria, who later saved the monarchy from the excesses of her male ancestors.

Edward's chief contribution to the park was the 1798 Martello Tower, named the Prince of Wales tower in his honour. Initially, Edward had trouble getting money from home, but convinced the British government that the French threat was imminent. With ten guns and in a position near the height of the land, Martello Tower covered the park. The trees around the fort were felled for clear sightlines. This tower was of a new design, based upon one that had almost stymied the British in Mortella, Corsica. It had very thick sloping walls that cannon balls could not penetrate.

PRINCE EDWARD, DUKE OF KENT, c.1805

THE MARTELLO TOWER, C.1870

The Martello Tower had a powder magazine in its bowels, with a cental shaft to haul up the bags, and sheltered two hundred soldiers. There was one weakness, however: a wooden roof. This was not corrected until much later. In 1862, the floors were strengthened and the circular storage area was divided into three bays holding 1,250 bags of explosives. New gun platforms adorned the concrete roof, and there was a normal garrison of eighteen.

THE NORTHWEST ARM BATTERY, 1863

With the beginning of the War of 1812, the Northwest Arm Battery was upgraded, and a shot-heating furnace was also installed. Meanwhile, the Point Pleasant Battery was being undermined by the sea. Parts near the water were abandoned and were rebuilt slightly further inland.

With the beginning of the American Civil War, a new semicircular battery, Cambridge, was started between the Tower and the Northwest Arm Battery. Fort Ogilvie was also completely rebuilt, as was York Redoubt across the Arm. Seven- and ten-inch cannons were installed behind massive earthworks covering concrete and brick fortifications and more trees were cut for sighting. Cambridge would not be finished until 1868.

In 1873, with the American Civil War and the Fenian threat past, the city signed a lease for the park for 999 years. The military still retained its rights to the forts. There were areas restricted to the public, including the Prince of Wales Tower, Point Pleasant Battery, and Cambridge Battery, while a nervous public kept away from the rifle range. Military technology forged ahead. Rifled cannons, which increased the range and accuracy of shells, had appeared during the 1860s. In 1888, breech-loading cannon appeared. Necessary improvements had to be incorporated in to the defence system. By 1896 the Martello Tower was no longer used as a magazine and was given to the William Smith family. During World War One, the tower again saw limited use as German prisoners were kept on the first level, right below the Smiths, creating a tense situation. Still, the family stayed until 1925.

**Gun Crew at
Fort Ogilvie,
c.1903**

By 1906 the British had left Canada and the Canadian army took over
Point Pleasant. The facilities were left in top condition, but Canada
quickly "economized," almost abandoning Cambridge and Fort Ogilvie
by leaving only guards at the batteries. World War One changed that.
By 1918 sixty-four men were living at the Ogilvie complex, too many
for the primitive sanitation. The well was often polluted, and the only
good water was two hundred metres away at a spring. Despite this, in
1920 married soldiers were stationed there. But by 1933, Ogilvie was
deserted, leaving no military presence in the park. Canada tried to
give the forts to the Point Pleasant Park Commission, but in the hard
times of the 1930s, the Commission did not have funds to make the
forts safe, and the military did not have enough money to complete the
job. The forts remained deserted except for Martello Tower, which was
turned over to the park commission in 1935.

World War Two reactivated the Point Pleasant batteries. Both Ogilvie and Point Pleasant sprang to life, Cambridge was fenced off, Point
Pleasant received a battery of searchlights, and Ogilvie's sanitation system was also upgraded. A constant supply of piped water and a paved
road from the Martello Tower, the tram terminal, appeared in 1940.
After the war, Ogilvie's twenty-four buildings were again used to house
military personnel. By the end of 1957, the military was gone, replaced
by park families. Cambridge and other military installations were partly
demolished in 1951, and only a public outcry stopped the complete destruction. But generally, the area was neglected. By 1959 the forts were
a disgrace while the military and the Park Commission debated over
responsibility. Progress was finally made in 1961 when Martello Tower
was declared a National Historic Site and preservations efforts began.
Today the park's forts are major tourist attractions, although little of
Cambridge is left and the steps to the top are not safe. The fort at Point
Pleasant is blocked off as the sea continues to undermine it. Martello
Tower is locked up, at least normally, but Ogilvie has ramparts that give
a fine view of the harbour.

At the end of World War Two, RCAF Gorsebrook broke the integrity of the Gorsebrook Golf Course when the Women's Air Corps residence was built on the northeast section of the field. By 1953 it expanded into a full air force residence with six somewhat austere concrete apartment buildings along both sides of the main road and a gym with an arched roof next to Gorsebrook School. The four-floor apartments had balconies and a central stairwell with a glass block exterior wall. Some held five families, others seven. The other major South End military residence was the Cathedral Barracks (Anderson Square), behind All Saints Cathedral. These barracks were originally part of the Convent of the Sacred Heart property. Located across College Street, the nuns referred to it as "Paradise." It was there that the nuns sheltered after the Halifax Explosion.

By World War Two, the barracks were owned by the Royal Canadian Army, who built the Cathedral Barracks to house their women's corps (CAWC). After the war, Dalhousie University rented some of the building for its nurses' residence. Then, in 1952, the Royal Canadian Air Force took over the area and renamed it Anderson Square in honour of the late Air Marshall N. R. Anderson, who was commander of Eastern Air Command from 1938 to 1942. Anderson Square had accommodation for officers and single airmen, served as the local reserve air control centre, and was the centre of the Halifax Air Cadets and the Supply Section. Its creation had been part of the Air Force's expansion, as Gorsebrook was no longer adequate.

The Navy League Building at the corner of Barrington and South streets was designed as a residence for merchant sailors, but later served as the air command centre for the Northwest Atlantic in World War Two. It was one of a series of clean, economical residences established by the Navy League to encourage the formation of a Canadian Merchant Marine. The cornerstone was laid by the Prince of Wales on his visit to Halifax on August 18, 1919. There was space for one hundred men and additional commercial space on Barrington. Built of reinforced concrete covered with yellow brick, it had a reading room, canteen and dining room, an officer's mess, and Nelson Hall, a seven-hundred-seat auditorium with an orchestra pit. The Barrington shops included Langille's Barber Shop and Henry Curtis Drugs.

In 1939 the Royal Canadian Air Force rented the building. Two years later they bought it outright. Here, they established the Eastern Air Command (EAC) for the Northwest Atlantic. This got off to a rough start given the rivalry between the Air Force and Navy. Initially, the EAC was not very efficient for a variety of reasons. Unlike the British Coastal Command, the Canadians had little experience in anti-submarine warfare. Canada also had trouble convincing both the British and Americans of their need for the latest bombers, bombers that would

close the mid-Atlantic gap where the U-boats had free play. Winter weather in the Northwest Atlantic was atrocious, much worse than in Britain. Finally, there was a tendency to play it safe by protecting convoys that needed little protection, while ignoring those that were likely to be attacked.

SUBMARINE NET FROM YORK REDOUBT TO MCNABS ISLAND, c.1940

But the Allies gained experience and Canada began building anti-submarine corvettes. The Allies were seeing results, but still, the Royal Canadian Air Force was behind. Between July 1942 and October 1943 the EAC only destroyed six U-boats. The other Allies took up the slack, so German Admiral Karl Donitz, with losses mounting all over the North Atlantic, for a time withdrew his wolf packs from the North American coast.

But the Germans were soon back. This gave the city quite a scare in the winter of 1944–45. First U-806 sank a liberty ship on December 21, 1944. On Christmas Day a German U-boat sank the destroyer HMCS *Clayoquot*, and another sub, U-1232, followed, sinking a number of ships off the coast of Nova Scotia in January, including two tankers. But German luck was about to run out. Arriving in the spring of 1945, U-886 had been detected by RCAF Canso bombers that tracked it for two weeks. In its desperate attempt to escape, the submarine ran south of Nova Scotia. On March 18th the U. S. Navy sank the sub. The U-boats struggled until the end and a few were still fighting off Nova Scotia when the Germans surrendered in May 1945. By the end of the war the RCAF had destroyed but twenty-one U-boats, or about nine percent of the Allied total. After the war, the RCAF used the Naval League Building as its central office and recruitment centre.

The 1917 explosion is very well-known as a North End event, but the
force of the explosion did not suddenly stop once it hit Citadel Hill.
The blinding flash that turned Richmond into a flattened wasteland,
that produced burning piles of wood where there were once homes, that
reduced steel and concrete factories to roofless skeletons and schools
and churches to shattered walls, killing almost two thousand, also
caused heavy damage in the downtown and South End areas.

Part of the blast may have been directed skyward by the frowning bulk
of Citadel Hill, but most of its effects were felt in the South End. Saint
Mary's Cathedral had its stained glass windows destroyed. They were not
replaceable until after the war, since they came from Germany. Up the
street, the Nova Scotia Technical College suffered a similar fate and the
Nova Scotia Museum, in the main building, had its display cases upset
and broken. Further up Spring Garden Road, the old brick Convent of
the Sacred Heart lost windows and suffered some structural damage. On
the other hand, the adjacent wooden College Street School only lost windows. Not so lucky was the brick Morris Street School, which was almost
destroyed, and was out of action for many months. The stairwells collapsed and a water tank on the roof came through the ceiling, just missing
the principal, H. H. Blois, in his office. All Saints Cathedral also lost its
stained glass and a crack formed along the north wall.

Even four miles from the blast in the deep South End, the stone
house of the superintendent of Point Pleasant Park suffered three
hundred dollars damage at a time when three hundred dollars was a lot.
Also, Pine Hill College, half a mile further west on Francklyn Street,
lost windows. Near the harbour, the Halifax Ladies' College was damaged and the dignified principal, Mrs. Trueman, was thrown from the

gymnasium stage as the windows came in. Even worse was the human toll in the South End, where twenty-one died.

Following the explosion, it was noted that the cold winter air shimmered due to the burning buildings. Glass was at a premium so blankets were often placed in window frames until the American Red Cross arrived with both glass and glaziers, as well as medical supplies, doctors, and nurses. Fortunately, the South End railway cut had been tracked, even though there was no proper terminal.

The South End hospitals were quickly repaired. Camp Hill Military Hospital on the South Common was brought back into action, helping to relieve some of the pressure on the Victoria General, the Children's Hospital, and the Halifax Infirmary. Temporary hospitals were established at Bellevue House on Spring Garden (sixty-six beds), and at the Waegwoltic Club (seventy beds), while Pine Hill College's 125-bed convalescent hospital was very useful. The South Street Poor House received a number of patients, while at the other end of the social spectrum, the Halifax Ladies' College held 153 beds. Most who were able to walk needed only dressing stations, like that established at the Convent of the Sacred Heart. A number of South End families took in orphaned or lost children.

Repairs took much time. When the Convent's regular students returned in January, they had to wear coats and gloves as the heat was not yet restored. The School for the Blind set up a free clinic with an American eye specialist. At the Armouries, the lineups were very long and the people never got warm, even inside. Camp Hill and the North and Central Commons also received many tents and later temporary homes. Despite mounting criticism, it would be 1923 before the last ones were torn down.

Schooling was also disrupted. With Morris Street School virtually destroyed, the students were assigned to the back shift (1:15 to 5:00 p.m.) at Tower Road School. Some students, however, did not return until their "community school" reopened. At Morris Street this was many months, since the repaired school was later used as a secondary hospital, taking patients from the Victoria General and the Halifax Infirmary. Meanwhile, the Halifax Ladies' College had been reopened in January 1918.

THE SECOND HALIFAX EXPLOSION, JULY 18, 1945

The Second Halifax Explosion, July 18–19, 1945, was potentially much worse than the first due to the presence of the super-explosive RDX at the Bedford magazine. The whole city might have been flattened but for the heroics of the naval firefighters who stood at the gates of hell battling the fire for twenty-four hours. Big blasts at 6:45 p.m. and 12:25 a.m. rocked the city. Damage far exceeded even the infamous VE Day Riot.

All residents north of Quinpool Road were ordered to leave, causing hopeless traffic jams at the narrow Arm Bridge. Others, mostly young, daring, and foolish, climbed Richmond Heights to view the fireworks. Many others walked to the South End, lost among the expensive houses they had perhaps never seen before. Many of the South Enders who did not leave spent the warm night sleeping in their backyards. A number of people also spent the night in Point Pleasant Park, on Dalhousie's Studley Field, or in the shelter of Collins Hill at the Gorsebrook Golf Course.

One South End resident, Margaret Martin, recalled that her mother was in Toronto with relatives. The reports led her mother to fear that both her daughter and husband, who was working at the Armouries, had been killed (in fact, both survived). During the first explosion,

Margaret had been playing tennis at the Waegwoltic; the players immediately dropped to the court. When she got home, the radio instructed Haligonians to open all windows. Margaret decided to stay in the house, hoping many blankets would absorb flying glass and other objects. Needless to say, she had a very uncomfortable July night, with her frightened dog shivering under the bed. The worst explosion came just after midnight. For the next week, the Waeg's tennis games were interrupted by people hitting the deck at any sharp noise.

The war over, the South End's military history virtually ended. The original seaward defences in Point Pleasant Park functioned until almost the end of the Second World War. During that conflict, the nerve centre for the North West Atlantic Command was in the Navy League Building at Barrington and South, while much of the post-war air force outside of Shearwater was housed for two generations at RCAF Gorsebrook and Anderson Square. Today, except for a few possible offices downtown, none of Halifax's defence is within the South End. But its legacy remains, especially in the old forts in Point Pleasant Park.

Chapter 9

Point Pleasant Park and Francklyn Park

THE GOLDEN GATES, C.1890

Point Pleasant Park is the largest forested area in the South End. Over time, it has become a slightly reduced, sanitized forest featuring a number of military sites and vistas of the harbour and the Northwest Arm. It remains more or less intact after having lost fourteen acres to the Ocean Terminals. Francklyn Park, adjacent to Point Pleasant on the Arm shore, never was a park, but rather an area with a number of estates that filled a number of roles including industry, recreation, and education, before settling on upper-middle-class housing.

Point Pleasant was Cornwallis's original site for Halifax, but after starting to clear the forest, he discovered the shallows and its exposure to southeast winds. Therefore, he built the town a few kilometres further north on the steep slope of Citadel Hill. The establishment of Point Pleasant as a park came about when certain Victorian civil and military officials became aware of a desire for a wooded area that was accessible from the city.

SIR WILLIAM YOUNG, C.1880

After erecting defences in the park during the U. S. Civil War, Lieutenant General Sir Charles Hastings Doyle had a more peaceful task. He oversaw the cutting of paths and drives and the removal of dead trees. In celebration of Halifax's 124th birthday, on June 23, 1873, the still-not-yet-finished park was opened. City council had agreed to an assessment of four thousand dollars the first year for completion, then an additional two thousand dollars yearly for the maintenance of the park. But it reneged, so an undoubtedly irritated William Young paid the first installment out of his own pocket. Young was one of the park commissioners along with the mayor, one alderman from each ward, and three citizens—John W. Ritchie, John H. Stairs and John Doull. Halifax, starved by too much tax-free land, still had trouble meeting its commitment. For example, in 1879, only $1,058 of the agreed-upon $2,000 was actually paid out.

PLEASANT STREET, c.1890

Young developed Point Pleasant Park and contributed the Golden Gates at the Young Avenue entrance (Young Avenue is named after him). In general, he volunteered many hours overseeing the work on the park. The gates were manufactured by the famous Starr Skate Company of Dartmouth. Young then added massive granite pillars to hang them. The later gatekeepers' lodge was also established at Young Avenue and was modelled on the gatehouse of the British Prime Minister, Benjamin Disraeli. It was expanded in 1944 with stone from Cambridge Battery.

The major roads leading to Point Pleasant were Tower and Pleasant. Tower led almost directly to the Martello Tower, while Pleasant went past Steel's Pond, a favourite skating area. The latter road tended to washout and skirted very close to the pond, sometimes with tragic results. This happened in January 1878 when two young girls, Amy Boutillier and Bella McDonald, and their driver, Alexander Wilson, drowned when their sled went through the ice. Still, the pond continued to attract skaters until most of it was lost to the Ocean Terminals. The last bit disappeared with the construction of the container pier.

QUARRY POND AND SUPERINTENDENT'S COTTAGE, C.1905 The supposedly bottomless Quarry Pond near the end of Young Avenue, used to supply stone for Fort Ogilvie, became a favourite skating area and place to sail model boats. This pond also saw tragic events. The 1889 suicide of the wife of George Harvey, head of the Victoria School of Art, was such an event. In despair, she kissed her children goodbye, walked to the park, and drowned herself in the pond. The Point Pleasant Park woods also attracted their share of problems. Babies, abandoned by desperate women, were sometimes found dead under piles of branches and leaves. In the 1870s several teenaged girls made the park their home. Supposedly from respectable homes, one was deported to England while the others served time here.

THE PURCELL
BOATHOUSE AT
POINT PLEASANT,
1882

Not only could Haligonians reach the park by road, but those on the western shore of the Arm could take the Purcell's Cove ferry. In 1853, a fisher from Purcell's Cove, Joseph Purcell, started a service using sail. He received a civic grant, and was allowed to lease a small plot in the park and build a waiting room. Not only did he carry passengers to and fro, he also transported troops to York Redoubt and carried the Royal Mail. Over the years, the family made a number of rescues. In later years, the Arm was patrolled regularly by the police.

In the early 1900s, the city built the Purcells a new house and landing slip at the park. The building cost a healthy $1,700, but rent was only one dollar per year and remained unchanged for years, until property tax increased to an arbitrary $298 in 1964. By then, the Purcells' motorboat averaged thirty passengers per trip on warm Saturday afternoons. The service, with five thousand total passengers in 1963, was a supplement to the transit service that ran as far as the Martello Tower.

Generation after generation of Purcells ran the ferry. But when Halifax tried to close the service in November 1963, public opposition killed the idea. Eight years later, in September 1971, the city finally closed the service. Aubrey Purcell's drowning that year while fishing was the precipitating event, although passenger numbers were declining. Today, the house site is a lonely cove with a marker to the family.

Swimming was once an important activity in Point Pleasant Park, but slowly declined due to increasing pollution. There was a fine sandy beach at Chain Rock in the extreme northwest of the park that had a bathhouse as early as 1915. Unfortunately, Chain Rock became an early victim of pollution when the city moved a sewer outflow nearby.

Black Rock on the harbour lasted longer. During World War Two, it was unusable due to the outfall from Fort Ogilvie, but with peace and the establishment of sanitation, the location became popular. The city changed the pebble beach to sand, installed changing rooms, and hired a lifeguard. The beach became popular due to bus access from Tower Road, but again, creeping pollution doomed it.

Martello Tower was the site of a near tragedy. This was the 1840 duel insisted on by lawyer John Haliburton against Joe Howe for comments Howe made in the legislature about Haliburton's father, Judge Brenton. Apparently the younger Haliburton had little sense of the principles of parliament, nor the sanctity of the law. Friends tried to dissuade the young fool, but he insisted. The two met outside the tower. Standing back to back, they walked fifty paces, counted by their seconds, and turned. At the drop of a handkerchief, they fired. Haliburton got his shot off first, trying to kill Howe, but missed. Howe, however, fired in the air, showing himself to be the better person. He said, "I will not deprive an ageing father of his son." Haliburton was lucky not to have been charged with attempted murder, jailed, and disbarred.

Point Pleasant is also the home of the Commonwealth, or Halifax, Monument. It overlooks the sea at the extreme end of the park. Originally, this was the site of the National Seaman's Monument, dedicated August 10, 1924, and transferred to the Citadel in 1954. The Halifax Monument, much more attractive, was unveiled on Remembrance Day, 1967. It lists the sailors, soldiers, and merchant seamen of Canada and Newfoundland lost at sea in both world wars.

THE ROYAL NOVA SCOTIA YACHT SQUADRON, C.1900

Before the Ocean Terminals forced it to move, the Royal Nova Scotia Yacht Squadron was located near Freshwater. Started in 1876, the squadron had a two-and-a-half-floor clubhouse built near the park in 1900. In 1922 the new Yacht Squadron headquarters were built on park land just inside the breakwater. The park commissioners protested the loss of land and received compensation, as they had when fourteen acres had been expropriated in 1913 for the Ocean Terminals. When the yacht club moved to the Arm in 1968, the park regained this small parcel of land.

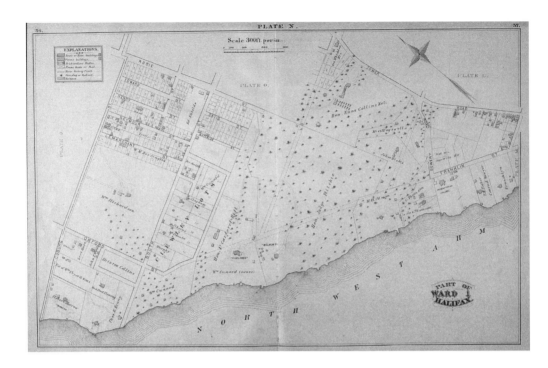

HOPKINS ATLAS, SHOWING FRANCKLYN PARK, 1878

Francklyn Park, adjacent to Point Pleasant on the Arm side, never was a true park. A semi-wooded area, it became exclusively residential after being a multi-purpose recreational, industrial, and residential area. It is located between Point Pleasant Park and the railway cut to the north.

EMSCOTE, C.1869   On the road between the Nova Scotia Penitentiary and Francklyn Park was the McCullough estate. On the other side lived the Francklyns (for whom the "park" and street were named) at their estate, "Emscote." The Francklyns were also a major force in establishing Saint Alban's Anglican Chapel on nearby Tower Road. F. H. Baker owned the next property, then there was Pine Hill College and the Thompson residences. Across the road, on Pine Hill, were a number of lots owned by the Cogswell estate.

**THE PROVINCIAL
PENITENTIARY,
c.1896**

The Provincial Penitentiary on the Arm was an estate unlike the others. It was based on the American, not British, model, and was designed after Auburn Prison, the chief prison in New York state. Consisting of fourteen acres on Francklyn Park's steep slope, it replaced the insecure lockup on Spring Garden Road. The cells were small and narrow—four feet by six feet. The cornerstone was laid June 24, 1841, and opening day was October 15, 1844.

Compared with the out-dated facility, Bridewell, the new penitentiary was far more secure. Escapes were still fairly frequent, though, and were occasionally violent. One desperate escapee, John Crosson, beat Captain Cameron, who had tried to capture him outside. But Crosson was subdued by a pitchfork-wielding farmer, who tied him to a tree to await the authorities. Much more serious was the riot of 1867. The guards at the time were described as feeble old men, so the opportunists took advantage. The governor called troops from Point Pleasant, who restored order only after shooting several still-defiant prisoners. In 1880 the males were transferred to the new federal prison at Dorchester. Chained two-by-two in distinctive yellow- and black-striped suits, they were transferred by horse-drawn buses to the North Street Station, then by train to New Brunswick's grim penitentiary. The few women left were soon released from the old prison. Paradoxically, the Anglican Church had a close relationship with the prison. At one point, the prison was examined as a possible source of granite for the proposed new cathedral at Robie and Coburg.

PINE HILL
DIVINITY COLLEGE
SHORTLY BEFORE
RAZING, C.1954

Pine Hill College, originally Presbyterian, became United in 1925 and then ecumenical in the late 1960s when the Catholics and Anglicans established their seminary there.

FERNWOOD,
c.1880

In 1927, there was only one house on the east side of Francklyn. This was the still-existing purple Victorian home of Donald and Mary Leverman at the corner of Point Pleasant Drive and Francklyn. On the west side, there were more, including "Fernwood" and "Maplewood," David McKeen's great Tuscan villa. The property owners in Francklyn Park had changed by 1951. The penitentiary was gone and development had started on those streets below Francklyn Street, including Chain Rock Drive and Inglewood. Here, dozen of upper-middle-class residences were erected in the 1950s on land sold by F. B. McCurdy.

Point Pleasant Park and Francklyn Park, which constitute the southern part of the peninsula, are now two entirely different types of property. Point Pleasant Park is a sanitized approximation of the original forest that covered Halifax. Francklyn Park is now a suburb for the upper-middle class.

Chapter 10

Hospitals and Universities

CITY AND PROVINCIAL HOSPITAL, BEFORE ADDITIONAL WINGS WERE BUILT, N.D.

The hospitals and universities are perhaps the most distinctive section of the South End. Central to the health and higher education of the city and province, they have, until recent years, been largely concentrated in the dozen blocks encompassed by Tower Road, Spring Garden Road and Coburg Road, Oxford Street, and South Street. South of this area is Saint Mary's University and east of it is the former Technical College of Nova Scotia and the former site of the Halifax Infirmary.

Although the City Hospital appeared on the South Common in May 1859, it was not the first hospital in the city, just the first public one. Following five years of agitation by the Halifax Medical Society, a promise of funding by the province, and money from the William Murdoch estate, the City Hospital was established. The building, brick with granite facings, cost thirty-eight thousand dollars, but was not opened regularly until 1867, when the province agreed to cover two-thirds of the operational cost and it became the City and Provincial Hospital.

The City and Provincial Hospital was allegedly a hard place to get into. A patient would have to get a certificate from the attending physician, then get more documentation from the doctor in "his quarter," present these to the Board of Charities in the Province Building downtown, a place that had short hours, a short staff, and short tempers. Finally, at the cost of a horse-taxi, the indigent patient would reach the hospital, only to find it filled with sailors. Because of its impoverished, diseased, and often dirty clientele, the lack of an understanding of infection, untrained and uncouth nurses, and no effective anaesthesia, the hospital did not gain the patronage of the middle class. The better-off were treated at home or went to private hospitals. They may have had their symptoms relieved, which was sometimes enough, but outside of a few diseases such as smallpox, doctors had little ability to cure disease. It was only with the acceptance of the germ theory, the development of safe and effective anaesthetics in the 1880s, and improvements in the nursing profession that the hospital became effective and the middle class appeared. In 1887, for Queen Victoria's Golden Jubilee, the City and Provincial Hospital changed its name to the Victoria General.

The name change in 1887 from the City and Provincial Hospital to the Victoria General also symbolized a change in the hospital's administration—from the city and province to the province alone. Much of the medical board resigned during the "Great Row of 1885" because of the Fielding government's interference in medical appointments. Now that that was largely solved, the hospital got back to business. In 1890, a nursing school was established and the first class graduated two years later, greatly raising medical standards. A pathology laboratory appeared at the VG in 1914, a decade after the X-ray machine was installed. The VG was now moving into an era of new technology.

In 1917 the Victoria General Hospital was damaged in the Halifax Explosion. Hundreds of windows were broken and the staff was overwhelmed for three or four days treating the injured under makeshift conditions. Fortunately, American military medical help arrived very quickly, staying some months to assist the overburdened staff. With repairs completed and the war almost over, the Spanish Flu attacked. Two months later, it disappeared, leaving many dead. Doctors would have no answers until the electron microscope revealed the virus. Wartime inflation, which meant food costs increased 142 percent between 1913 and 1919, created budgeting problems. Still, the VG opened a private pavilion for the genteel in 1921, featuring better care and a more hotel-like atmosphere.

The 1920s brought the controversy over the appointment of Dr. Harold "Benge" Atlee as gynecologist at the VG. This holder of a military cross from the Gallipoli disaster was a controversial social democratic, very young but very experienced in the ways of the world. Atlee soon proved his medical critics wrong, even if they despised his freely given opinions on socialism. The 1930s meant more careful budgeting. Still, in 1932 the cancer clinic was established, and several good medical graduates found positions at the hospital. But the charity load was very heavy, encouraging a new building.

VICTORIA GENERAL HOSPITAL, C.1955

The fourteen-floor Victoria General opened in 1948. Four years later, the new nurses' residence and nursing school opened. Also, antibiotics such as penicillin came on stream at the end of the war, helping reduce infection. The outpatients unit started in 1949, replacing the century and half service of the Halifax Dispensary. But there was no socialized medicine so patients were either free (if on welfare), or forced to pay, in part or in full, for services.

The Poor House on South Street at Robie was, for many, the bane of the South End. An overcrowded and poorly ventilated Poor House was originally on Spring Garden Road's north side, with its graveyard, which dated back to 1780–81, in Grafton Park.

The newer Poor House building at South Street was to be "a noble monument to charity and benevolence," both spacious and airy. Designed by local well-known architect David Stirling to resist fire, the fireproof basement kitchen was not fully implemented. The home cost $112,396.69, shared by the city and province. Finished December 1, 1869, the Poor House was a combination of an old-age home, an asylum for poor families, a minor hospital, a refuge for the mentally and physically disabled, and a place for inebriates. The latter group defined the place for too many, although most were mentally ill.

Even with a new building, there were problems with the staff. In 1870 a number of nurses became drunk and rioted. The director, Edward Shields, enlisted the help of male residents to lock them up. One of the leaders received four years in Rockhead Prison. On the other hand, healthy residents were sometimes employed on road work, cutting stone, or picking oakum or old rope to pieces. But there never was enough work. Only the children had some chance of escaping, as they received an elementary education.

Director Edward Shields died in 1880 after forty years service. He was replaced by William Fleming, who spurned the help offered by Shields's daughter, the matron. This was a fatal error, for on the night of November 6, 1882, the dreadful "Midnight Fire" broke out in the kitchen. Initially thought to be suppressed, it soon flared up and travelled to the roof through the ventilation shaft added after the building had been completed.

Of the 343 inmates, 31 died. Most of the blame was placed on Fleming, who was assumed to be incompetent. The survivors were temporarily housed in the barn and other outbuildings before arrangements were made to house them in the recently abandoned penitentiary on the Arm. This was unsuitable, but would be their home until the building was rebuilt in 1886. The survivors received army cots and blankets, but overflowed the one hundred cells, spilling into the corridors. Others received shelter from friends and relatives, while some ended up on the streets and probably drifted into a life of crime. The stronger inmates were later employed to tear down their ruined home. They were seen trudging back and forth from Tower Road to the site where they lost their few possessions, where they had lost their friends and relatives, and almost, their lives. The Royal Army Engineers finished the demolition job with gun cotton.

A third Poor House was opened in the same location on South Street
in October 1886. This time fire resistance was implemented. It had a
maximum of four floors, but was spread out over three wings. It cost
over one hundred thousand dollars to build, of which almost half came
from insurance on the old building. When, in 1886–87, the city took
over the full administration of the Poor House, the province took responsibility for the adjacent City and Provincial Hospital.

By 1913 Dalhousie's Forrest Campus was becoming crowded, and
the university started searching for a new area. They soon considered
the Poor House property. This would solve two problems—the college would gain much-needed space and the city would rid itself of the
unsightly institution. A new Poor House was to be built near the old Infectious Hospital overlooking the Bedford Basin. But at the last minute,
Dalhousie received a better deal on the old Murray estate, Studley. The
Poor House stayed, unwanted and unloved, for almost sixty more years
until it was demolished in 1972.

HALIFAX MEDICAL
COLLEGE, N.D.

Travelling down Morris on the south side and crossing Robie, there was Fire Station no. 3 (1908), then the cottage-style TB Hospital (1921) and Infectious Disease Hospital (1928). In winter, the old Infectious Disease Hospital at Rockhead was often inaccessible and poorly heated. It was finally decided to build the new hospital on Morris Street, next to the TB Hospital, but in early 1927 Halifax was still in a post-war recession and mayor Joseph B. Kenny thought the $95,000 cost of a new building too high. The medical profession disagreed, pressing for an efficient place to treat infected patients before disease spread into the community, as cholera had in the 1830s. Council agreed; Kenny resigned. The final cost of the building was $110,000.

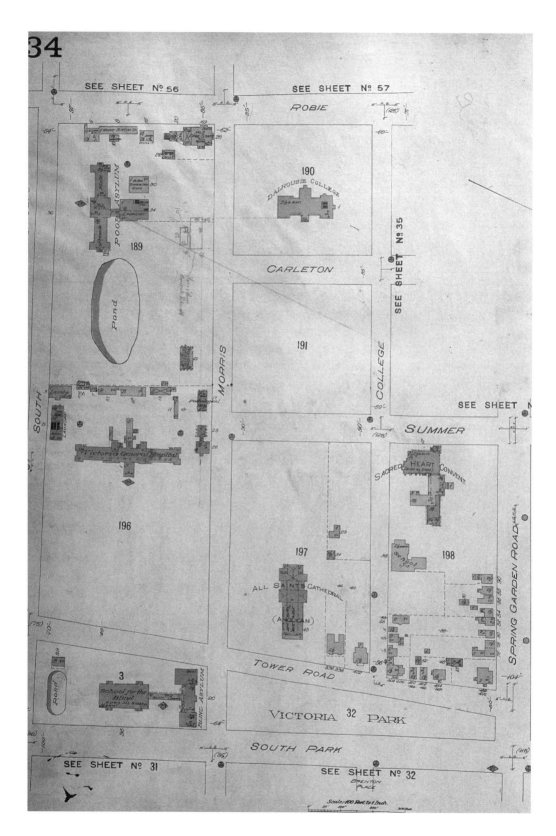

In the last half of the nineteenth century and early twentieth century institutions started appearing along Morris west of South Park. On the south side was the School for the Blind (1871), while across Tower, the City and Provincial Hospital (1859) and All Saints Cathedral (1910) appeared. By the 1920s institutions were appearing toward Robie. On the north side, the 1927 City Directory shows the Grace Maternity Hospital (1922) at Summer Street. Then came the Dalhousie Public Heath Clinic (1924) with the visiting dispensary at Carleton and Morris. Next was Dalhousie University with the Forrest Building. Continuing across Robie, there was an un-boulevarded section all the way to LeMarchant Street, where houses blocked direct entrance to the Studley campus. The Halifax Medical College on College Street was at one time the home to Dalhousie's medical school, and would later rejoin the university.

Near to the new Infectious Disease Hospital were the Children's Hospital (1909) and the Pathological Institute of the Victoria General Hospital (1914). South Street has the VG's Private Pavilion at Wellington, and up the street at South and Robie is the Poor House.

The Camp Hill Military Hospital was established in temporary buildings on Camp Hill in 1917. When, in the 1920s, there were complaints of smoke from a chimney placed too low, these original buildings were replaced by a well-remembered brick one. For many years, except for the construction of Queen Elizabeth High School next door in 1942, there was no change. The arrival of the Abbey Lane Hospital in 1972 started the development of the Camp Hill Hospital zone. Today, there are two hospital zones in the South End—the older one on University Avenue and the newer, smaller, but more prominent one on Camp Hill.

Halifax had religious hospitals, too. The Halifax Infirmary was started by the Sisters of Charity on Barrington and Salter Streets in 1887. In 1933 it was rebuilt on Queen Street in yellow brick. The metal crucified Christ on the side of the new wing was the most prominent feature. In the 1990s, the Infirmary was replaced by the new secularized Infirmary at Camp Hill. Only the nurses' residence on Morris survived.

DALHOUSIE, 1834. BUILDING AT THE GRAND PARADE WITH THE TANDEM CLUB OUTSIDE. Dalhousie University goes back much further than the Studley campus, occupied only since 1913. Originally, it was in the downtown area at the site of the modern-day City Hall, and later, in the Forrest Building at the corner of University (then Morris) and Robie. In the William Edgar painting above, the original Dalhousie building, once a cholera hospital, is shown at Grand Parade.

FORREST BUILDING, DALHOUSIE, c.1890

Founded on the nonsectarian principles of the University of Edinburgh, Dalhousie quickly foundered—not once, but twice. First, it was tested on its non-sectarianism and found wanting. The college refused to honour its commitment to hire Edmund Crawley, a Baptist, as professor. The outraged Baptists founded Acadia University in Wolfville in 1839, spawning a series of small sectarian colleges so lamented by the Victorians. The other problem was that Dalhousie had trouble getting provincial funding in a colony that only supported colleges on denominational criteria. Dalhousie, being non-sectarian, was accused of being "Godless." It was declared dead—twice. But the college kept frustrating its critics by resurrecting itself. The college did not get off the ground until 1863 when it finally offered degrees. By this time there were already three small, provincially funded sectarian colleges: Acadia (1839), Saint Mary's (1839), and Saint Francis Xavier (1855).

Eventually, the province funded Dalhousie, too. With additional private money, which started to arrive in the 1870s, Dalhousie became the unofficial provincial university. With its teachers secure and with the machinations and contributions of Sir William Young, Dal sold its Grand Parade site and opened the Forrest Building, seven years *after* Nova Scotia ended support to all its colleges on December 31, 1880. Soon the denominational colleges were sending their best students to Dal for professional degrees.

In 1913 Dalhousie received a deal on the Studley campus, so moved its arts and science faculties there, keeping the Forrest Building for medicine and law. First to appear on Studley were the MacDonald Library and the Science Building. The post-war period saw Studley begin filling in. Shirreff Hall, the big women's residence, was completed with a generous three-hundred-thousand-dollar donation by Jennie Eddy (née Shirreff). Then, except for the move by the University of King's College to the northwest quadrant of the campus in October 1930, little was built during the Great Depression. By this time, Dalhousie had a campus largely defined by a central quadrangle, with the old Murray homestead at its head, the library and science buildings on the north side, and the administration building on the south. The campus was graced by paths shaded by elms and maples. The buildings were a comfortable fit for the 753 undergraduates.

DALHOUSIE'S STUDLEY CAMPUS, c.1932

The big academic event of the 1920s was the Carnegie Corporation's attempt to do what the Nova Scotia government had failed to do two generations earlier—create an efficient, central, provincial university. Dalhousie was to be the site. Negotiations dragged on against great resistance that even a five-hundred-thousand-dollar offer to each of the other colleges to relocate to Dal could not overcome. Ultimately, only King's College, burned in 1920 by children playing with matches, moved.

NOVA SCOTIA TECHNICAL COLLEGE, N.D. Opened September 28, 1909, the Nova Scotia Technical College on Spring Garden Road was also taken over by Dalhousie and now offers engineering degrees through the university.

The 1930s were particularly tough on Dalhousie and the other colleges. But Dal did as well as any. Most students were from upper-middle-class families, some from the wealthy and a few from the working class. As the Depression continued, the total number of enrolled students plunged from 1,015 in 1932–33 to 846 in 1937–38. The rich were able to continue sending their sons and daughters almost as if nothing had happened, but the bourgeoisie were struggling. The result was that fewer daughters were educated in favour of sons, who had a better chance of finding suitable employment. The construction of the big A and A building in 1951 meant the end of the Murray homestead, but gave space for a faculty of Graduate Studies and relieved the overcrowding caused by returning veterans. Soon the university benefited from increased government funding and took over much of University Avenue, eventually linking the Studley and Carleton campuses.

UNIVERSITY OF KING'S COLLEGE RESIDENCE, BIRCHDALE, 1931

The University of King's College, one of Canada's oldest, was the dream of Bishop Charles Inglis. He first established it in Windsor, Nova Scotia, far from the temptations of the city. Modelled after Oxford, King's unfortunately imposed the Thirty-Nine Articles on graduates, despite Inglis's objections. The articles insulted Catholics by not having enough sacraments and many Protestants by having any at all. This imposition had been engineered by none other than Alexander Croke, a member of the King's board of governors. When King's opened, almost no one arrived.

The university struggled onward, favoured by both the colonial and home governments, causing more resentment. Eventually the British government cut its extra funding and King's dropped the Thirty-Nine Articles and tried to establish itself as the provincial university. The Anglicans seemed incapable of doing what the Presbyterians had done for Dalhousie; King's was going nowhere. Therefore, several plans were made to unify with rapidly growing Dalhousie. Only the disastrous 1920 fire finally forced the proud but impoverished King's to join. The Carnegie Corporation came to the rescue, offering King's six hundred thousand dollars if the institution could come up with four hundred thousand dollars. This was a struggle, but with the help of the parishes, King's succeeded and reestablished itself on the northwest quadrant of Studley.

University of King's College, 1930

By coming to Studley as a constituent college of Dalhousie, King's agreed to hold its degrees in abeyance, with the exception of theology. This was a bitter choice. Eventually the proud college accepted its fate, developed some fine professors and its own specialized courses, increasingly drawing Dalhousie undergraduates. World War Two was harder on King's than on Dal. King's lost its campus to the Navy and students were housed at Pine Hill and took their classes at Dal.

Saint Mary's University, which formed the same year and for similar sectarian reasons as Acadia, initially was located on Grafton Street. It offered both degrees and theological training leading to ordination. The first classes opened in January 1839. The first degree seems to have been given in 1843, a generation ahead of Dalhousie.

The local Catholic elite brought Irish priests to run the institution. The rector, Rev. Doctor Richard Baptist O'Brien, became well-known locally. He lectured at the Literary Society, at the Mechanic's Institute, and to Catholic groups. O'Brien's departure in 1845 produced an outpouring of grief and his subsequent career in Britain and Ireland made the local press many years later. The college and seminary had an outlook that was typical of the time, with a strong indoctrinary bias. Contemporaries noted that there were many more young students than at other colleges.

Saint Mary's got its first real campus in 1868 when it moved to Belle Air on North Street. Here it became the second college in the North End, joining the Presbyterian Free Church College on Gerrish. Neither of these would stay for long. Saint Mary's closed in 1883 as a result of the province cutting funding to post-secondary education. For two decades, there was no local post-secondary education for Catholic men.

Archbishop Edward McCarthy, a graduate of Belle Air College, reopened the college in 1913 on Windsor Street. He brought in the Irish Christian Brothers and obtained the eighty-thousand-dollar Power Estate. Unfortunately, the brothers were unable to raise the general level of the college enough to have their second-year students automatically admitted to Dalhousie. But they got their second-year men admitted to the Nova Scotia Technical College. Individuals from the campus did make it to Dalhousie's law and medical schools, but on their own. McCarthy's successors thought the Christian Bothers had obtained too generous an agreement and tried to get rid of them. Archbishop John T. McNally succeeded. The Christian Brothers left in 1940 rather than accept tight control. McNally then brought in the Jesuits and in 1951 opened a new campus at Gorsebrook.

SAINT MARY'S UNIVERSITY, c.1955

The same year that Saint Mary's rose from the golf course, Mount Saint Vincent burned to the ground. The Sisters of Charity offered to buy ten acres of Gorsebrook and establish a women's college on the Saint Mary's campus. They were denied. The Jesuits and archbishop would have no thin edge of feminism penetrating the heart of Catholic male education. Eventually, all this would change, and finally, in the 1960s, Saint Mary's started admitting women.

Selected Bibliography

Akins, Thomas B. *History of Halifax City*. 1895. Reprint. Dartmouth: Brook Hill Press, 2002.

Blakeley, Phyllis R. *Glimpses of Halifax*. Reprint. Belleville, Ontario: Mika Publishing, 1973.

Doyle, W A B. *Creation of a National Air Force,* Vol 2." Toronto: The University of Toronto Press, 1986.

Erickson, Paul A. *Historic North End Halifax*. Halifax: Nimbus Publishing, 2004.

Fingard, Judith, Guildford, Janet, Sutherland, David. *Halifax, the First 250 Years*. Halifax: Formac Publishing, 1999.

Forbes. E.R. *The Atlantic Provinces in Confederation*. Toronto: University of Toronto Press, 1977.

Henry, Cynthia, editor. *Remembering the Capitol Theatre, 1930-1974*. Halifax: Atlantic Black Book, 2000.

Marquis, Greg. *In Armageddon's Shadow : The Civil War and Canada's Maritime Provinces*. Montreal: McGill-Queen's University Press, 1998.

Markham, Susan Evelyn. *Investigation on the Development of Commons of Halifax, NS 1749-1979*. Halifax: Dalhousie University, Graduate Studies, History MA, 1980.

Raddall, Thomas H. *Halifax, Warden of the North*. rev. ed. Halifax: Nimbus, 1993.

Waite, Peter B. *The Lives of Dalhousie University*, Volume One, 1818-1925." Montreal, Quebec: McGill-Queen's University Press. 1994. Volume Two. 1925-1980." Montreal: McGill-Queen's University Press, 1998.

Watts, Heather and Raymond, Michele, *Halifax's Northwest Arm, an illustrated history*. Halifax: Formac Publishing, 2003.

Image Sources

With the exception of those listed below, all images have been supplied courtesy of the Nova Scotia Archives and Records Management. Numbers correspond to page numbers in the book.

Courtesy of the Dalhousie University Archives Photographic Collection (PC1 35.22.9): 63

Courtesy of the Dalhousie University Archives Photographic Collection (PC1 14.1): 169

Allan Dunlop: 107

Bill Mont: 98

Black Cultural Centre: 61

Library and Archives Canada: 4, 42, 46, 62, 109, 119, 140, 166

Mary McNab: 95

Mills Brothers: 31

Nova Scotia Sport Hall of Fame: 108, 128

Public Archives of Canada: 8

Saint Mary's University: 102

Wilfred Creighton: 96

Index

W

Waegwoltic Boat Club 121, 129–130

Wanderers Grounds 40

Water Street 11

Weir, Benjamin 17

Wentworth, Governor John 8, 9

White, Portia 60–61

Woods, Reverend James 40

World War II 62, 63, 89

Worrell, Bishop Clarendon 75

Wright, George 79

Y

Young, Sir William 54, 80, 146, 147

Young Avenue 79, 80, 147